Calm and in Control

Simple and Effective Strategies to Support Young Children's Self-Regulation

Julie Tourigny, OTD, MS, OTR/L

www.gryphonhouse.com

Copyright

Published by Gryphon House, Inc.
P. O. Box 10, Lewisville, NC 27023
800.638.0928; 877.638.7576 [fax]
Visit us on the web at www.gryphonhouse.com.

Library of Congress Control Number: 2023932094

Bulk Purchase

Gryphon House books are available for special premiums and sales promotions as well as for fund-raising use. Special editions or book excerpts also can be created to specifications. For details, call 800.638.0928.

Disclaimer

Gryphon House, Inc., cannot be held responsible for damage, mishap, or injury incurred during the use of or because of activities in this book. Appropriate and reasonable caution and adult supervision of children involved in activities and corresponding to the age and capability of each child involved are recommended at all times. Do not leave children unattended at any time. Observe safety and caution at all times.

Dedication

To my children, Ian, Teddy, and Josie, who have encouraged me through this project with their enthusiasm and endless curiosity.

And to my husband, David, for always believing in and being there for me.

Table of Contents

Acknowledgments ..... **v**

Introduction **1**

Chapter 1: What Self-Regulation Is and Why It Matters **5**

Chapter 2: Self-Regulation and Executive Function **21**

Chapter 3: Sensory Play throughout the Day **33**

Chapter 4: The Self-Regulated Preschool or Pre-K Classroom **47**

Chapter 5: The Self-Regulated Kindergarten Classroom **57**

Chapter 6: Calm during Mealtimes **69**

Chapter 7: In Control during Circle Time **85**

Chapter 8: Calm and in Control While Learning **97**

References and Recommended Reading **105**

Index **108**

Acknowledgments

Over the past two decades, countless mentors, educators, colleagues, family, and friends have influenced my work in a way that has made this book possible. I am grateful for each of you and the impact you've had on me as a professional and a person.

I would like to thank the occupational therapists and speech and language pathologists at the Colorado Center for Pediatric Learning and Development who have greatly influenced my thinking and my work with children and their families. Their dedication and talent for bettering the lives of the children with whom they work has been an endless source of inspiration for me.

Introduction

Hello, early childhood educators! Do you have children who just can't seem to manage their emotions? Who can't seem to sit still? Who'd rather get a laugh from a classmate than pay attention? These children may be struggling with self-regulation. This book is designed to provide simple yet effective sensory strategies and activities to help you teach your children how to regulate their emotions and behaviors during the school day.

Self-regulation is the ability to remain calm and in control of our thoughts, actions, and emotions in response to an external event or stimulus. It helps us stay on task and focus on what is relevant. It helps us control our impulses and body movements, no matter how excited, angry, or upset we become. It helps us match our behavior and social interactions to the situation. The better we are at self-regulation, the more successful we will be at life's tasks.

As adults, our ability to self-regulate supports us throughout the day. When completing tasks such as running errands or keeping the house clean, we are using self-regulation so we can engage in activities we need to do instead of activities we would likely prefer to do. Remaining calm after someone cuts us off on the highway or slips into a parking spot we were about to take also demonstrates self-regulation skills.

Self-regulation is not something we are born with. It is a skill we learn and improve upon over time. Most children learn to self-regulate between the ages of three and seven (Montroy et al., 2016). Before this, infants and toddlers rely on co-regulation. *Co-regulation* refers to the nurturing interactions young children have with familiar adults who provide the support, modeling, and training they need to "understand, express, and modulate their thoughts, feelings, and behaviors" (Murray, Rosanbaum, Christopoulos, and Hamoudi, 2015). These supportive interactions promote the development of strong self-regulation skills.

As with many skills, young children will demonstrate a wide range of self-regulation abilities. Preschool, kindergarten, and even first-grade children require support to develop these skills. Some children need help recognizing that something is upsetting or overly exciting. Others may have difficulty knowing how to calm down and take control of their emotions or behaviors on their own.

In the classroom, children with emerging or poorly developed self-regulation may struggle with sustained attention, impulse control, and social interactions. Consider these examples.

Jeffrey, a five-year-old kindergarten student, sits down with his classmates for lunch. He's already eaten his favorite things from his lunch box during snack time. The remaining foods are healthy choices that do not interest him. When a peer pulls a treat from his lunch box, Jeffrey demands that he share the snack. The peer says no and starts to open the snack, but Jeffrey grabs and smashes it. The peer seeks out an adult for support, describing what just happened. Jeffrey begins to yell and cry, saying, "He wouldn't share with me!" Jeffrey exhibits poor self-regulation that affects his impulse control and social interactions.

During circle time, a four-year-old prekindergartner tells a joke. The whole class and the teacher laugh. To help refocus the class, the teacher claps her hands three times, awaiting the same response from the children. Next, Matteo takes a turn, but instead of sharing, he acts silly, rolling around and saying nonsense words to get the group to laugh again. The teacher tries to shift his attention so he will focus on circle time, but he continues in this manner. Matteo exhibits poor self-regulation that affects his impulse control and his ability to shift from a silly moment back to circle time.

Maya, a kindergartner, has spent most of center time talking with her friend. When her teacher gives the class a five-minute warning, she has yet to start on her project. The teacher gives the class a three-minute warning and then a one-minute warning. Maya ignores these cues and continues to talk. When the teacher tells the class that it is time to clean up and get ready for outdoor recess, Maya becomes upset, saying that she hasn't finished her project yet. She disrupts the class by refusing to clean up and affects their transition to outdoor recess. Maya exhibits poor self-regulation first when she chooses to ignore her center-time project to socialize with her peers and again when she resists the transition to recess.

How to Use This Book

There are many sensory strategies that support self-regulation. Providing a nurturing and consistent school environment rich in sensory play and activities helps develop self-regulation skills in all children. *Calm and in Control* describes these sensory strategies, explaining when to implement them and how to create an environment that supports all children as they navigate learning, social interactions, and impulse control throughout the school day. In *Calm and in Control*, I explore techniques to support:

- Turn-taking
- Sharing
- Lining up as a group and coping with not being first in line
- The ability to refrain from blurting out answers
- Freedom from separation anxiety
- The ability to handle transitions
- Regrouping after something funny happens
- Impulse control
- Socially appropriate behavior

Refer to *Calm and in Control* often for ideas on enriching the school day with sensory activities and strategies that prevent disruptive behaviors. The book will help develop self-regulation skills for every student in your classroom.

Let's get started!

Chapter 1:

What Self-Regulation Is and Why It Matters

What Is Self-Regulation?

Self-regulation is the ability to remain calm and in control of thoughts, feelings, and actions, especially in response to something that elicits a strong emotion. It is a foundational life skill that affects our interactions, friendships, and overall well-being. Children who are well regulated can control their behaviors and emotions in a variety of situations, even when they feel overwhelmed, angry, frustrated, or overexcited. This allows them to get along with their peers, demonstrate patience while learning how to cooperate with others, manage their negative emotions, and maintain their focus on activities even when challenges arise.

Well-regulated children are better at:

- developing and maintaining friendships;
- learning, remembering, and following classroom rules and routines;
- learning and playing independently;
- problem solving;
- persisting with an activity even when it is frustrating or difficult; and
- performing to the best of their ability in school.

Children who struggle with self-regulation exhibit challenging behaviors that are often disruptive to the entire classroom. They may:

- quit difficult games and activities;
- sabotage activities when they feel frustrated or angry;
- become angry or upset quickly and struggle to calm down on their own;
- disrupt the class with overly silly or impulsive behavior; or
- demand attention from caregivers to help them finish a game or activity.

Children who frequently experience intense emotions that result in withdrawal, tantrums, or overly silly behaviors may be having difficulty regulating themselves. They are unable to cope with their feelings appropriately. Many young children have not learned how to handle the strong emotions they feel in response to new events, foods, or activities. These children may act impulsively, destructively, or aggressively. Their behaviors are a sign that they need support.

How Self-Regulation Develops

Infants and toddlers largely rely on co-regulation with a caregiver to understand the world and manage their emotions. Gradually, they begin to self-regulate as they interact with people and objects. Newborns are almost completely reliant on caregivers to meet their physical and emotional needs for food and comfort, soothing, safety and survival, and transitions from asleep to awake and awake to asleep. Infants co-regulate with caregivers to meet their emotional needs. With time and consistency, they begin to develop self-regulatory behaviors such as waiting to be picked up, to receive a bottle, to have a diaper changed, and to regulate their temperature. They learn to calm and sooth themselves. Toddlers begin to self-regulate some of the time but still rely on co-regulation to manage most of their actions and reactions.

Young children rely less on co-regulation and are able to self-regulate more often. However, they continue to require co-regulation to manage big emotions in new situations. Because this shift from co-regulation to self-regulation occurs during the toddler and younger childhood years, young children need many opportunities to learn and practice self-regulation. The more they do, the more likely they are to develop strong regulation skills they can rely on throughout their lives.

Older children and teenagers self-regulate most of the time, but co-regulation is still necessary, especially in difficult social situations. By early adulthood, the need for co-regulation has diminished, as individuals rely almost entirely on self-regulation skills to think, act, and react.

Young adults should be able to self-regulate almost all the time. However, throughout one's lifespan, people rely on co-regulation to work through difficult social and emotional situations.

The Range of Self-Regulation Skills in Early Childhood

As self-regulation increases, the need for co-regulation decreases. The time at which this shift occurs will differ from child to child based on temperament, home life, stressors, and prior experiences. Some children will enter preschool or kindergarten with limited self-regulation skills; others will have no difficulty remaining calm and in control throughout the school day.

Depending on their early experiences with co-regulation, young children exhibit a wide range of regulation abilities when negotiating conflict, taking turns, sharing limited resources, and talking respectfully to peers and teachers. For example, children without siblings may have fewer opportunities to work on social skills at home. They may lack any understanding of social norms and will push, bite, and steal toys to get what they want. Some children will react to new situations fearfully, refusing to engage, crying, or having a tantrum. Other children may have no tolerance for frustration when an activity is difficult for them. They will become overly upset with themselves or the activity itself, breaking and throwing things.

Although each of these behaviors can be challenging for caregivers, they are normal in young children. The good news is that children have the ability to:

- learn strategies for remaining calm and in control of their feelings;
- replace challenging behaviors with adaptive ones; and
- interact with their peers in socially acceptable ways.

Teaching Self-Regulation in the Classroom

Often, one or two children who exhibit challenging behaviors, such as tantrums, blurting, fidgeting, withdrawal, shyness, or an inability to follow directions, can dictate the energy and overall mood of a classroom. Behaviors such as these are disruptive and distracting to the entire class. When teachers react to these behaviors with punishment, the child receives attention, albeit negative, which may reinforce the negative behavior instead of diminishing it.

To help children learn more adaptive ways to manage their feelings, actions, and reactions, create a nurturing environment marked by:

- Consistent classroom rules and routines
- Opportunities to learn about feelings
- Modeling of self-regulation skills
- Practice of self-regulation skills through open-ended sensory play

In a classroom environment where self-regulation is seen as a skill that needs to be discussed and developed, children can learn appropriate and adaptive responses to difficult feelings or social situations. Each time they experience strong emotions, they will have new tools to maintain a calm demeanor and remain in control of their reactions.

Consistent Classroom Routines and Rules

When establishing classroom rules, discuss the rules of the class as a group. Give examples of what following the rules looks like, and allow the children to ask questions. Discuss disruptive behaviors, and give examples of what those might look like. Post visual aids that depict the rules throughout the classroom, and teach nonverbal cues to help redirect children. Include the children in the development of any additional rules.

A consistent classroom schedule and routine creates an environment that promotes self-regulation skills. When children know what to expect out of their day, they tend to be calmer and more in control of their emotions. For example, when the morning routine begins with free play, followed by circle time, then snack, followed by outdoor recess, children understand what they should be doing and what they will be doing next. This predictability provides them with a sense of control, which makes transitions go smoothly, and decreases disruptive behaviors.

Consistent classroom routines also exist within activities. When children arrive at school, they sign in, place their jackets and backpacks in their cubbies, and wash their hands. During morning circle time, establish a routine such as the following:

- Teacher greets the class
- Teacher talks about the class schedule and reminds children of the classroom rules
- Children share something with the class
- Teacher reads a book

During afternoon circle time, establish a routine such as the following:

- Teacher discusses positive things she observed during the school day
- Children share positive things they observed
- Teacher reads a book

Although the circle-time routine should remain relatively the same each day, the length of time may vary. Be careful not to run circle time for too long. To make the most of this important time of the school day, plan to spend five to fifteen minutes engaged in a combination of passive and active learning activities. Depending on the age of the children and their attention span each day, circle time could vary in length, but it should last only as long as the majority of children are engaged. There will be days when the class is having difficulty paying attention and circle time will end early. And there may be days when the class remains actively engaged and circle time may extend beyond fifteen minutes.

Teaching Children to Identify Feelings

Often, young children's strong feelings are invalidated by caregivers, who may mean well. Children may hear statements such as, "Stop crying," "There's no reason to be so mad," or "Calm down." These reactive statements do little to stop children from feeling the way they do in the moment and do not prevent them from feeling this way again in the future. While children may recognize that caregivers disapprove of their behaviors, they will continue to get mad, cry, and act out if they lack the tools to replace those behaviors with an adaptive response.

One of the best ways to help children manage their feelings is to teach them how to identify feelings. While they read books, watch shows, and engage in school activities, label and talk about feelings. That way, they will learn to name and understand their feelings, especially strong ones. Then, they can develop a toolbox for replacing big emotional reactions with regulated, calm responses. To nurture these skills, caregivers can substitute:

"I see that you are upset right now," for "Stop crying."

"I can tell that you are mad right now," for "Don't get so angry."

"I see that you are really frustrated," for "Calm down."

Caregivers who use statements such as, "Kayla, I can see that you feel mad because someone took your toy," validate what children are feeling. Continuing the conversation with suggestions for an adaptive response will help children learn to be well-regulated. For example, an extension of the statement might be, "Kayla, it is okay to feel frustrated that Joey took your toy. It is not okay to hit him or throw things." This validates how Kayla is feeling and also lets her know that she should not violate the rules of the classroom when she is mad.

Teaching children about the emotions they are experiencing and suggesting appropriate reactions will diminish challenging behaviors over time. Children who have learned about feelings should be encouraged to practice identifying them when they arise and when they encounter them in stories. The purpose of identifying feelings is to develop self-awareness as well as the ability to understand what another person is experiencing. Once children can identify their feelings, they should be encouraged to practice pausing and reflecting on the emotion. This introspection helps them understand why they are feeling a certain way. Then, they are ready to practice adaptive responses.

Replacing Dysregulated Responses with Regulated Ones

Acting out, whether it is avoidance, withdrawal, yelling, fleeing, or being overly silly, is a maladaptive response to a thought or feeling. Children rarely act out for no reason. An important aspect of self-regulation is the ability to be self-aware. When children are self-aware, they are able to recognize how they are feeling and why.

Before learning self-regulation skills, many children react to unfamiliar situations with a fight-or-flight response. This is especially true during times of stress or intense emotions. The response may prevent children from remaining calm and thinking before they act. The frustrated child may push, break or throw things, hide, cry, or refuse to engage in classroom routines. When children experience something new, whether it is a sound, a taste, or how a thing looks, it may cause a big feeling, such as fear, anger, or overexcitement.

These dysregulated reactions are a result of children's internalizing or externalizing their feelings. Children who internalize their feelings may react with:

- Withdrawal and hiding
- Sullenness
- Refusing to interact with peers
- Abandoning games and activities

When children externalize their feelings, they may react with:

- Bullying
- Blaming
- Lashing out at peers
- Aggressive behavior
- Demanding attention

Teaching children that they have a choice about their reactions is another important part of developing self-regulation skills. They will learn to recognize when they have a choice, identify the emotions they are feeling, pause before they react, and use new strategies to help them calm down and remain in control of their thoughts and actions. In this stage of the process, children are learning about how they tend to respond to a big feeling. They also learn that they have control over how they react.

> Charlie loves to be the center of attention. He seeks opportunities to tell jokes, laugh, and socialize with his friends. He is curious and engaged in all classroom activixties. However, Charlie struggles to wait his turn. He often blurts out the answer instead of waiting to be called on. He pushes to the front of the line during transitions and demands one-on-one attention from the teacher when she is working with other children. When he does not get his way, Charlie becomes upset and struggles to calm down. Charlie's teacher helps him learn that he cannot always be the first in line or the first to answer a question. She is helping him learn to be patient and to control his impulsivity.

Once children can identify their feelings, understand why they feel the way they do, and pause to think about how they want to respond based on established classroom rules and social norms, they are ready to learn appropriate responses. Caregivers are now in a position to provide children with options to support a self-regulated response. Children have gained self-awareness, which will help them confidently regulate their emotions in a wide variety of situations. They will learn that it is okay to feel strongly, to pause before they react, and to think about the following:

- What am I feeling right now?
- What made me feel this way?
- What do I want to do?
- Is it appropriate?
- What have I learned how to do instead?

At first, children may rely on the guidance of a familiar and nurturing adult to accomplish these goals. Consider the following examples. Sammy always cries when her parents drop her off in the classroom. She stands in the doorway and refuses to participate in the classroom routine, such as placing her backpack and jacket in her cubby, washing her hands, and joining her classmates in free play. Sammy's teacher can support her by acknowledging that she is feeling sad. He can help her identify that she is sad because she misses her parents. He can help her understand that she is crying because she feels sad. Finally, he can let her know that it is okay to feel sad and even cry for a bit, but that she still has to put her things in her cubby, wash her hands, and join her classmates.

Levi, a kindergartner, often throws and breaks toys when he feels frustrated. In preschool, he was frequently punished for this behavior, getting time-outs or being denied the opportunity to play with his favorite toys. His kindergarten teacher, however, notices that his motor skills are somewhat delayed. When he doesn't feel successful at an activity, he quickly becomes frustrated and acts out. Instead of punishing Levi, his teacher tries to help him regulate his emotions. While the class draws self-portraits, she spends extra time supporting Levi. When she notices him becoming upset, she sits down next to him and says, "Levi, it looks like you are frustrated right now." She gives him the language to identify the feeling he is experiencing, then she teaches him how to identify why he might be feeling that way. "Levi, it looks like you are upset that your drawing is not turning out the way you want it to. This is making you feel frustrated." Next, in a calm voice and without patronizing him, she says, "Levi, even though you are frustrated, you may not throw or break the crayons." She may even give a reason why he is not allowed to throw and break crayons, such as, "If you break the crayons, by the end of the year there won't be any left," or "If you throw your crayon, it could hit someone and hurt them." Finally, Levi's teacher provides him with alternative and adaptive responses to his frustration.

Fostering an Environment Where Children Practice Self-Regulation

Practicing self-regulation through play allows children to work on this important skill without the threat of failing or making a mistake. By creating an environment where children can experience a feeling, pause their reaction to think about how they should respond, and remain calm before reacting, the teacher develops a classroom of well-regulated children. Exposure to stimuli that cause big reactions, such as a messy hand, an unexpected noise, or a stolen toy, provides young children with opportunities to learn to regulate their emotions. Children with poor self-regulation will feel intensely and react intensely. Well-regulated children may still feel intensely, but they will be able to pause and react in a calm and adaptive way. These practice opportunities help children develop foresight, which is extremely important for good self-regulation. Play allows children to stay calm and in control of their feelings by using a toolbox of self-regulatory strategies.

Sensory Sensitivity

Sensory play helps children learn that they have control over their response to big feelings. When a big feeling arises during play, caregivers can guide children through it, encouraging adaptive responses such as using their words, cleaning their hands when they get messy, or engaging in calming self-talk. For example, engaging in open-ended sensory play—play that has no end point and is enriched with sensory opportunities—lets children experience a range of motor, social, and emotional conflicts. When there is no end point or desired outcome, children can focus on learning how to control their actions and behaviors while engaged with peers. Enriching the classroom with sensory play activities and strategies throughout the school day encourages children to develop strong self-regulation skills.

Chloe does not like it when her hands get dirty. She tends to avoid messy foods such as pudding and messy activities such as fingerpainting. She becomes very upset and disrupts the class by crying and running away whenever messy items get on her hands or clothes. She also spends most of snack and mealtimes worried and not socializing with her classmates. Chloe's teacher observes that crying and avoidance are her only go-to strategies.

One morning, the teacher fills a few small sensory bins with shaving cream. She places plastic animals in the bins, covering them with the shaving cream. Alongside the bins, she places spoons, shovels, a sprayer filled with water, water bottles, and paper towels. When it's time for free play, she describes the activity to the children, letting them know that they will be going on a treasure hunt to search for lost animals. She demonstrates for the children how they can look for the lost animals with their hands, a spoon, or a shovel, and then talks about how using a shovel or spoon keeps her hands dry while she searches. When she finds an animal, she uses the spray bottle to clean off the shaving cream and dries the animal with a paper towel, talking about how it was full of shaving cream but is now clean and dry.

Chloe's classmates crowd around the bins, digging, searching, and cleaning the animals. At first, Chloe refuses even to go near the activity. Her teacher points out that some children use the shovels to scoop out the animals, thereby keeping their hands clean, and that others pour water over the animals to clean off the shaving cream and then dry them with a paper towel. She suggests that Chloe practice some of these techniques the next time she encounters something messy. Chloe nods but chooses to read a book instead of searching for animals.

For the rest of the week, Chloe's teacher continues with the treasure hunt, hiding new things each day. One morning, the hidden objects are ocean-themed: shells, sea creatures, and plastic mermaids. Chloe loves mermaids and decides she'd like to try to search for one. Her teacher sees her interest and lets her know that if her hands get messy, she can quickly wipe them clean with a paper towel or rinse them off with the water. This gives Chloe an opportunity to practice making a regulated response to a feeling she dislikes while engaged in a highly desired activity.

Fine- and Gross-Motor Skills

Many children struggle with frustration, embarrassment, and anger while they are learning something new. Those who are still developing their fine- and gross-motor skills may overreact when they aren't successful with an activity. These children must practice both their motor skills and their self-regulation skills because they become overly frustrated when they make mistakes. They may sabotage or abandon the activity to avoid feeling that they've failed. Encouraging fine- and gross-motor skill development through sensory play helps children gain confidence and stick with the activity even when they make mistakes. In open-ended sensory play, the stakes aren't high because there is not a winner or loser or a right or wrong way to play.

Jernell is a messy eater. He struggles to open milk and juice boxes, often spilling the liquids on himself or the table. He is clumsy eating with a spoon and fork and makes lots of messes. The children at his table talk about how messy he is and sometimes laugh at him. This makes Jernell act out, throwing his food, refusing to eat, and even hitting his peers. Jernell's classroom teacher realizes that he would benefit from practice with scooping, pouring, using utensils, and opening his food and drinks. She sets up a sensory table in the classroom filled with toy utensils, cups, and bowls. She makes the play kitchen a center activity and encourages the children to pretend they are chefs cooking meals. While she has designed these activities with Jernell in mind, all the children will benefit from the motor opportunities. She reminds the children that it is okay if they spill and make mistakes, and she urges them to have fun. Jernell is able to scoop, pour, mix, and use utensils while practicing how to regulate his emotional response to frustration.

Modeling Self-Regulation

Infants, toddlers, and young children learn to navigate the world around them by imitating the emotions and reactions they see in familiar adults and caregivers. Older children who lack self-regulation skills often copy the responses they see in their caregivers. Adults who are calm and in control of their emotions demonstrate to the children around them how they regulate their emotions. When caregivers consistently respond in big, angry, or overreactive ways, children can mimic these actions and fail to develop successful self-regulation. Guiding children to respond calmly to intense feelings or stimuli will help combat dysregulation and challenging behaviors. Such guidance will lay a foundation for improved self-regulation the next time they encounter these stressors. In contrast, punishment, scolding, and impatience may cause children to believe that their overactive reactions are justified. This will likely lead to prolonged behavioral issues and classroom-management problems. When teachers and caregivers act calm and in control, they set an example for children and confirm that this is the proper behavior. Modeling self-regulation is a valuable tool to help children learn adaptive ways to react when they feel sad.

When Chloe is upset during mealtimes, Ms. Johnson, Chloe's teacher, sits next to her. She allows a bit of the yogurt she is eating to dribble onto her hand, pointing it out to the children at the table. She acknowledges that she doesn't really like how the yogurt feels on her hand, describing it as cold and wet. Ms. Johnson also states that she wishes the yogurt hadn't spilled on her, but she knows accidents happen. She then explains, "Whenever I eat, I keep a napkin near me. That way, when I spill something, I can just clean it up. I don't like the way the yogurt feels on my hand, but I know I can wipe it off and the yucky feeling will go away." Ms. Johnson has explicitly stated how messy hands make her feel. Then, she describes and demonstrates a strategy, using a napkin to wipe it off, to give Chloe an option to calmly deal with messy foods.

During free-choice time one morning, Ms. Williams sits with Levi while he plays with blocks. She builds a tower and lets it tumble over while she is still constructing. As she picks up the fallen blocks, Ms. Williams states, "When I mess something up that I'm working hard at, it really frustrates me." She starts to rebuild the tower carefully and says, "I take some deep breaths and remind myself that it's okay to make mistakes." As she takes a few deep breaths, Ms. Williams keeps building carefully and continues talking, "I tell myself that it's okay and then I try again." Ms. Williams then asks Levi if he wants to help her build. As they build together, she exclaims, "Even though the tower I was building just fell down, I'm going to try again. I hope I build it taller this time." Ms. Williams has modeled for Levi that everybody makes mistakes, and she explicitly stated that mistakes feel frustrating to her. She demonstrated deep breathing and showed Levi that she tries again in hope that the next time she will build the tower even higher.

Another modeling strategy to help children learn self-regulation skills is role-playing. Role-play is an excellent strategy to model self-regulation skills with children who struggle with impulse control and patience.

Charlie's teacher's aide, Ms. Marquez, asks him if he'd like to help her run circle time. Charlie enthusiastically agrees, so she suggests that they practice. Ms. Marquez asks if he could be the teacher and she will be the student. They gather up a few classmates and move over to the circle area. Charlie sits in the teacher's chair while the aide and his classmates sit on the carpet. Charlie runs the mock circle time (with prompts from Ms. Marquez when needed), asking questions and calling on his classmates and his aide. At times, Ms. Marquez acts impatient and overly eager to answer questions, talking over the children and blurting answers. When they finish, Ms. Marquez and Charlie talk together about what it was like for him to be the teacher, how it felt to have to call on just one student to answer questions and share, and, finally, how Charlie felt when she blurted and interrupted so that she could answer first. Ms. Marquez hopes that the role-play experience will help Charlie realize that he can't always be called on because every student in the class deserves a chance to answer and share.

Modeling self-regulation through demonstration, role-playing, and storytelling helps children learn strategies they can use to remain calm and in control of their feelings when they feel sad, overwhelmed, frustrated, angry, and impatient. When teachers define and describe their own emotions and model adaptive responses, children learn to recognize and respond to their big feelings in similar ways.

Self-regulation—the ability to remain calm and in control of thoughts, actions, and emotions in response to an external event or stimulus—helps children stay on task and focus on what is relevant, control impulses and body movements, no matter how excited, angry, or upset they become. This skill is not present at birth. Rather, self-regulation is learned and improves over time with practice and maturation. Considering that most children learn to self-regulate between the ages of three and seven, there is an opportunity to teach this important life skill in the early childhood classroom. Providing a nurturing and consistent school environment that is rich in sensory play and activities helps all children learn to be well-regulated. Through modeling, teaching the children to identify feelings and emotions, and open-ended sensory play, children learn adaptive ways to manage their feelings, actions, and reactions, all of which will benefit their social, emotional, and academic performance.

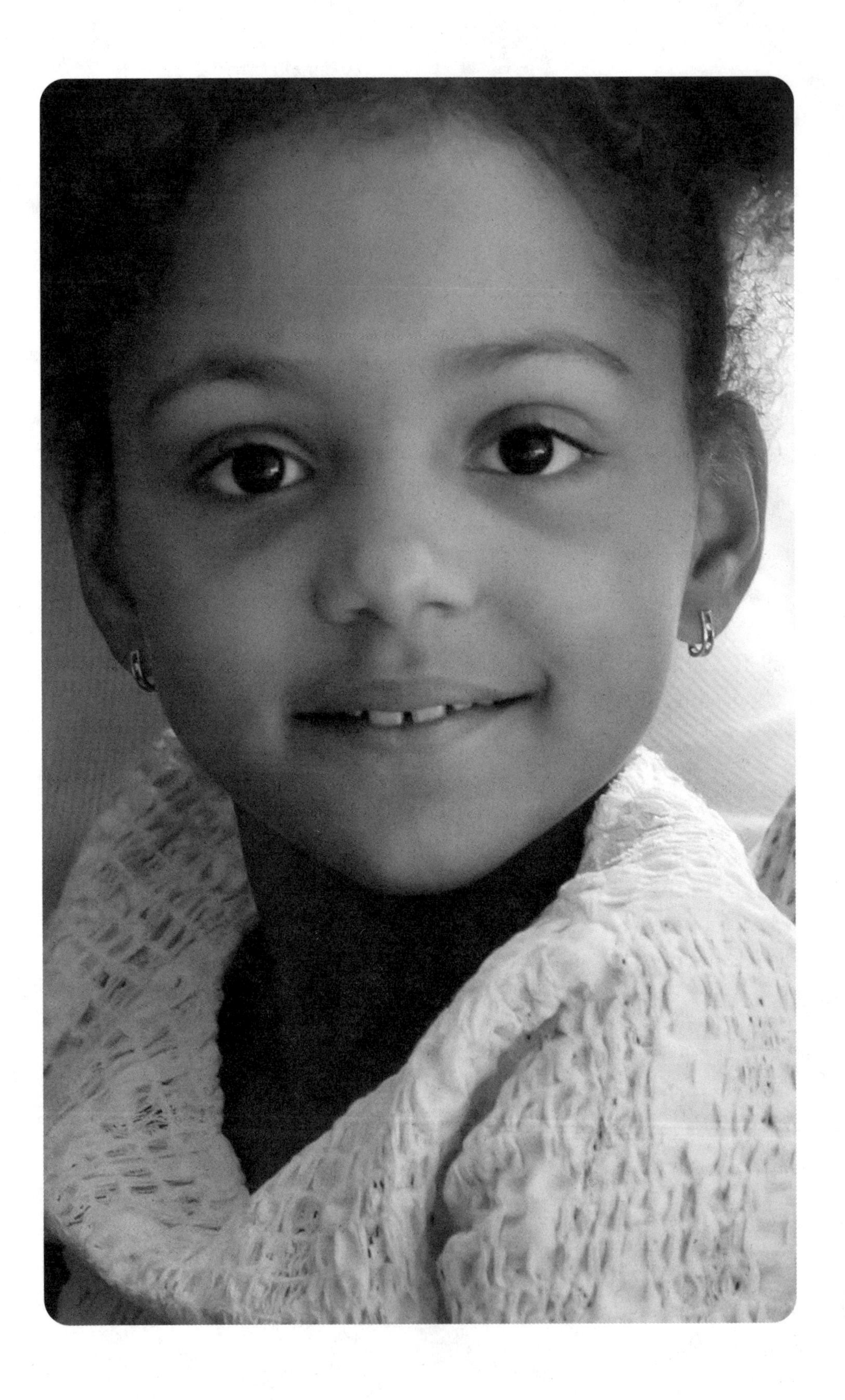

Chapter 2:

Self-Regulation and Executive Function

Older children and adults regularly engage in activities that are automatic, unconscious, and require no attentional effort, such as using utensils to feed ourselves, riding a bicycle, and typing. However, at one point these skills were new to each person and needed to be learned and practiced. In addition to learning these types of complex motor skills, young children have to learn to remember things that are important, such as the classroom rules and routines. They need to learn to pay attention to what is important and block out irrelevant sights and sounds going on around them. They need to learn to control their impulses and behaviors as they develop appropriate social-emotional skills. These attending, memory, and impulse-control skills—called *executive function*—guide children's ability to learn new skills. Throughout the school day, children rely on executive functioning to successfully engage in activities, socialize with peers, transition from activity to activity, and eat meals and snacks. How well children are able to complete these activities is largely dependent on their self-regulation skills. When they are well-regulated, children can draw upon their executive-function skills to stop, think, and then act.

Executive function is a group of mental skills that includes attentional flexibility, working memory, and self-control. While these three skills are different from one another, children rely on all three to set a goal, plan the steps required, and then sustain attention to focus on and complete a task. Executive function is also responsible for:

- Transition skills
- Word and idea generation
- Taking turns with a desired toy
- Remembering multistep directions and following them in the correct sequence
- Sustaining attention to start and finish projects
- Problem solving
- Organization skills
- Self-monitoring
- Regulating emotions
- Understanding other people's points of view

Children need strong executive-function *and* self-regulation skills so that they can think before they act, consider the consequences of their actions, and make an appropriate response. Well-regulated children demonstrate this pairing in many ways. For example, when they want to play with a highly desired toy during center time, the well-regulated child is able to stop and ask for what they want rather than cry, lash out, or throw a tantrum. They are able to inhibit their desire to cheat and patiently wait for their turn while playing games with classmates. They pay attention during a story rather than acting out or interacting with children around them. They wait in line without pushing or shoving. They remain calm and in control and try a challenging task without demanding assistance from a peer or the classroom teacher. Rather than give up or abandon challenging learning activities, they follow through to the end of an activity, even when it is hard or frustrating.

Attentional Flexibility

Attentional flexibility is one of the three main executive functions. It is the ability to switch focus from one task or activity to another when it is appropriate to do so. This flexibility allows children to pay attention to a specific task or person talking as they tune out irrelevant information. Children with age-appropriate attentional flexibility are able to pay attention to what they are supposed to and also remain open to the possibility that something else, such as a fire alarm or a spilled drink, may require them to quickly shift their attention.

Attentional flexibility also allows children to filter or tune out incoming information that is not important to them. In the classroom setting, these are typically visual and auditory distractions, such as a person passing by in the hallway, activity going on outside, or fans spinning overhead.

When children can't filter out extraneous stimuli, their attention wanders between the activity they are engaged in and background noises and sights they should ignore. Children rely on attentional flexibility to sustain their focus on a given activity, a friend talking to them, or the teacher's instruction, regardless of distractions occurring around them.

Flexible and Inflexible Thinking

Flexible thinking, the ability to think about things in a new or different way, is a type of attentional flexibility. Flexible thinking allows children to play a game a new way, accept another person's point of view, and problem solve new or challenging activities. Children who can think flexibly are adaptable and able to tolerate changes in the schedule, a classroom disruption, or a classmate who has a different way of playing a game. Many children have no trouble adjusting to change because they are flexible thinkers. However, children who struggle with attentional flexibility, especially those who are not well-regulated, may become overly upset at changes to the routine or have difficulty accepting another person's point of view. Inflexible thinking is a maladaptive pattern that has a negative effect on children's success both academically and socially. Even with a predictable classroom schedule and routine, the school day is constantly changing, and children encounter situations that require attentional flexibility. For example, people may enter the classroom while on a tour of the school, or a fire drill may occur. Children who are well-regulated and have intact attentional flexibility can accept changes to the schedule and move on with their day.

When children struggle with attentional flexibility, they may seem rigid in their thoughts. They need the routine to stay the same, often do not want to try new games or activities, and may struggle with problem solving. Children who are not flexible thinkers may have difficulty remaining calm and in control of their emotions at school, and they may become frustrated when the classroom routine changes, peers don't follow the rules or suggest new ways to play a game, or things don't go the way they want them to.

> Anthony, an outgoing kindergartner, is playing with peers during free-choice time. He and a couple of friends are building a complex road-and-city system using wooden blocks and cars. When it is time to drive the cars along the roadways and through the city, they discover that one car, the group's favorite, is missing. The well-regulated children in the group with intact attentional flexibility choose a different car and continue to play together. Anthony, however, cannot stop thinking about the missing car, even with other options present. He refuses to choose a different car to play with and acts out by destroying a part of the city he and his peers had created.

Ruminating thoughts are another type of inflexible thinking. Children who ruminate over something have difficulty focusing on the activity at hand because they are thinking too much about a what-if scenario.

> Serena, a three-year-old preschooler, doesn't like it when her hands get dirty. During circle time, when her classroom teacher describes an upcoming center-time activity involving fingerpaint, glitter, pompoms, and glue, Serena begins to fidget and is noticeably distracted. When it's time for centers to start, Serena begins to cry and refuses to join her peers. Not only was Serena unable to focus during circle time, but she is also not able to control her emotions to transition to center time, because just the thought of gluing and fingerpainting makes her upset.

With some support and guidance, children can improve their attentional flexibility, especially in an environment where they are learning self-regulation skills. Serena's teacher works with her throughout the year, helping her identify her feelings when she thinks about having messy hands. During sensory play activities, the teacher provides her with coping strategies, such as having a towel close by to wipe her hands or using paintbrushes to keep her hands away from the paint. Over time, Serena learns that she can control her thoughts about messy play. She often engages in these activities for a shorter amount of time than her peers, and she almost always uses a paintbrush or popsicle stick to move paint around, but she pays attention to the activities, regulates her emotions, and experiences pride in her art. By the end of the school year, Serena can create a fingerpainted Mother's Day project that she is proud of, without having a tantrum or meltdown.

Working Memory

Working memory, the second main executive-function skill, is the ability to keep relevant information in mind for as long as it is needed. It is a type of short-term memory that holds onto information needed in the moment to complete a given task or set of tasks.

Different from long-term memory, working memory refers to the small amount of important information children need to retain to successfully engage in cognitive tasks and classroom activities. Children use working-memory skills to follow classroom rules and routines, complete new activities, and follow multistep directions. When children struggle with working memory, they may lack the ability to independently follow established classroom routines.

Zaylee is a happy and energetic four-year-old who attends half-day preschool four days per week. On entering the classroom, she removes her coat and backpack and tosses them on the floor. She avoids the sign-in center and rushes right to the pretend play area, her favorite part of the classroom. When Mr. Lee, the classroom aide, reminds her that she must put her things in her cubby and

> sign in before she can play, she ignores him and keeps playing. When he cues her again, she looks up and exclaims, "I will later. I'm playing right now." Mr. Lee responds, "Remember in our classroom the rule is, first we sign in and then we can play." Ignoring him, Zaylee continues to play. After a moment, Mr. Lee says, "Zaylee, it's not time to play right now. Now, it's time to put your things in your cubby and sign in. That way everyone will know you're here today! And, Ms. Spring will know that she can choose you for one of the classroom jobs!" Zaylee again refuses, even with the positive spin Mr. Lee has put on the importance of signing in. Finally, Mr. Lee states more firmly, "Zaylee, this is not a choice right now." Zaylee shouts, "No!" and begins to cry.

It is important to remember that young children have limited capacity to retain information and call it up when needed, but as they gain more experience with working memory and as they mature, their ability to retain larger amounts of information increases. For example, a toddler will do well with two-step tasks: "First, go get your shoes. Then, we will get in the car and go." However, she may not be able to retain a more complex set of instructions, such as, "First get your shoes, then get your toy, and then meet me at the back door so we can go." An older child will be better able to retain this more complex list and successfully meet her caregiver at the back door with both her shoes and her favorite toy. It's important to recognize the limitations of children's working memory based on age and experience and to avoid requiring them to remember too many rules or difficult routines. This will support them in succeeding at what they are capable of remembering.

Preschool-aged children may need visual cues and verbal reminders to successfully complete the classroom morning routine as they transition from home to school. Many will need support to remember to first place their things in their cubby, then wash their hands, and finally sign in. In contrast, kindergartners should be able to remember that when they arrive at school they need to place their things in their cubby, remove any homework or important things needed from their backpack, place their lunch where it belongs, sign in, and transition to the first classroom activity. They should be able to remember to complete each of these steps with few cues or reminders as they are better able to retain a larger amount of information.

Self-regulation has a great effect on working memory, either supporting successful memory retention or undermining this important cognitive ability. When children are well regulated, they are calm and in control and have the capacity to remember, retain, and act on what they need to to successfully follow the rules and routines of the classroom and to complete new tasks and activities. Children who are not well regulated may lack the ability to focus and attend to what is being said to them or what they should be doing. These children will require reminders, cues, and assistance to remember and follow through with established classroom routines. They will need help to remember the directions already given to complete activities and class work.

Filtering

Young children are still learning about what is relevant and irrelevant. When they focus too much on irrelevant information, their working memory can become cluttered, diminishing their ability to retain the information they need. Classrooms that are noisy or cluttered with materials may hinder children from accessing necessary information in their working memory during activities and in social situations. In this type of distracting environment, children who struggle with self-regulation may become overwhelmed when asked to recall directions, classroom routines, and rules. A classroom that has few unnecessary auditory distractions, that children can move around and navigate materials easily, and that looks neat and organized, will support children's ability to attend and focus. An organized classroom will decrease children's needs to filter out irrelevant information and will help them listen and pay attention.

Working Memory and Self-Regulation

Self-regulation supports working memory skills in the classroom because well-regulated children will have more capacity to draw upon the established rules and expectations while they are engaged in activities and social situations. Intense emotions such as excitement, anger, fear, and frustration may diminish working memory. When children feel intensely and then react intensely, they are unable to participate in the established routines. Creating an environment that is free from unnecessary visual and auditory distractions, has clearly defined and discussed classroom rules, and follows a predictable routine, will support working memory skills.

Strong self-regulation skills provide a foundation for children to be able to not only learn *how* to remember but also *what* to remember. Once children can do this, they are able to draw upon what they've saved in their working memory to complete tasks.

> Geoff's parents have recently divorced. He is struggling with this change and splitting his time between two homes. Although his mom and dad are coparenting well, Geoff sometimes comes to school ready to learn but has been having really tough days when he cannot seem to pay attention or focus. He is quick to anger, lashing out at other children on some days, or crying over seemingly small things on others. On the days when Geoff is struggling to remain in control of his emotions, he has a hard time paying attention during circle time and needs a lot of support to complete his classwork. Instead of working on what he should be doing, he stares out the window, listens for activity in the hallway, and fidgets in his seat. His classroom teacher, Ms. Miles, recognizes these difficulties and tries to alleviate some of the extraneous distractions in the classroom to support his ability to pay attention and remember directions. During circle time, she has Geoff sit close to her and far away from the front door. She asks him to repeat directions back to her, encouraging him to "be the teacher" to help him retain instructions. These small adjustments decrease distractions and help Geoff attend to what he should so that he can remember what he needs to be successful.

Inhibitory Control

Inhibitory control, the third main executive function, is the ability to attend to what matters instead of what is unimportant or irrelevant. It is also the ability to inhibit behaviors to maintain self-control. Young children use inhibitory control regularly in the classroom when they refrain from blurting out an answer, grabbing a toy instead of waiting their turn, and pushing to the front instead of standing in their place in line. Children with strong inhibitory control can wait their turn, control their impulses, and persist at activities. They attend to what their teacher is saying or engage in a conversation with a friend while blocking out the unimportant visual and auditory events happening all around them.

Children who struggle with inhibitory control may act impulsively, ignoring the classroom rules and established social norms to get what they want right when they want it. They may overreact when games and activities don't go their way and throw tantrums when they don't get what they want. Their work may be rushed because they may be easily distracted and tend to focus on everything going on around them. Some children may act impulsively throughout the day.

Other children are able to control their impulsive behavior most of the time or for most of the day before they start to act out.

> Damon is a curious and engaged kindergartener who starts each day ready to learn. He is energetic, asks good questions, and is always focused on each lesson. He's quick to respond to questions and loves to help out. He is kind to his friends and easily follows the rules and routines of the classroom. His mother reports the he "goes at 100 miles per hour and then crashes." She further reports that on the weekend and school holidays he still takes a nap. While Damon doesn't seem tired in the afternoons, Ms. Shalynn, the classroom teacher, notices that he has trouble controlling his impulses. During afternoon circle time, he tends to struggle to keep his body quiet. He also tends to blurt out answers to questions Ms. Shalynn asks, preventing his classmates from answering. When he does wait to be called

on, he cries or becomes visibly upset when he is not chosen. Some days, Ms. Shalynn thinks it's as if Damon acts like two completely different children.

Attentional Inhibition

Attentional inhibition, or selective attention, is the brain's ability to focus on something important while tuning out other visual and auditory stimuli. Children must inhibit attending to visual and auditory distractions while listening to the teacher as she gives instructions for a seated activity. They must learn to attend to their classwork while surrounded by classmates who might be coughing or sneezing, fidgeting in their seats, or walking around the classroom. They must inhibit their attention to what is going on in the hallway or outside their window to maintain focus on the task at hand, such as lunch, play, or work. When children have a conversation with their peers, inhibitory control helps them focus on what the peer is saying instead of all the other conversations and noises in the classroom.

Response Inhibition

Response inhibition is the ability to suppress inappropriate behaviors. It is a type of self-control that supports goal-driven behavior. Children who struggle with response inhibition in the classroom may:

- rush their schoolwork;
- blurt answers without waiting to be called on;
- disregard the classroom rules and routines when they want something badly;
- write or say the first answer that comes to mind without thinking it through;
- throw a tantrum when they do not get what they want right when they want it: or
- struggle with patience and waiting their turn.

When the stakes are high and children really want to succeed in an activity such as winning a board game or answering a question, they need strong self-regulation skills combined with attentional flexibility to prevent maladaptive responses, such as blurting, cheating, aggressive behavior, or sabotage, from ruining their social interactions. A child who is intensely focused on winning may neglect the rules of the classroom. A child eager to answer a question may take over the conversation and blurt answers without allowing other children to show what they know. This child may lack both the attentional flexibility and self-regulation to recognize that the rules of the classroom and social norms supersede winning. Children who are well regulated will be able to remain calm and in control of their feelings even when they really want something.

Inhibitory Control and Self-Regulation

Self-regulation supports inhibitory control so that children are able to maintain control over their impulses and desires without overreacting when they are not able to get what they want when they want it. Remaining patient is challenging for many young children, especially when they really want to win a game, blurt out an answer, or be first in line. Children need to be well regulated to remain calm and in control of their thoughts and actions.

Self-regulation and executive-function skills help children decide how to behave and lead to strong academic and social skills. The three components of executive function—working memory, attentional flexibility, and inhibitory control—are distinct from one another but work together. Well-regulated children with intact executive-function skills can control their impulses and remember to use a more appropriate response, all while remaining calm and in control of their thoughts, feelings, and actions. Children rely on executive function skills to pay attention, remember new information and store it for the next time it is needed, control their impulses, and make an adaptive, calm response. A classroom that supports strong self-regulation skills will help children learn, remember, and focus on what they need to when they need to, so that they are able to socialize and learn to the best of their ability.

Chapter 3:

Sensory Play throughout the Day

Play is the job of children. It is a primary way they learn about the world. Play fosters creativity, improves fine- and gross-motor skills, enhances social skills, and cultivates self-regulation. When children play, they master skills without the threat of failure. They learn to take turns, how to share limited resources, how to communicate, and what to do when they encounter something they don't like. Through play, children improve both their executive function and self-regulation skills (Hofmann, Schmeichel, and Baddeley, 2012).

Open-ended sensory play involves activities that engage children's senses of balance and movement, sight, sound, taste, touch, and smell. This type of play helps them develop a strong awareness and understanding of the world around them. Open-ended play means there is no set end point or purpose, which gives children the freedom to play without the threat of failure. This prolonged engagement enhances focus and satisfaction and may encourage children to stay with the activity longer than they otherwise might.

Through open-ended sensory play, children learn self-regulation skills that, with a little encouragement from a nurturing caregiver, can be easily transferred to other parts of the day. Sensory components in an activity enhance learning exponentially. Studies show that sensory play helps children calm down when they feel anxious, overwhelmed, or angry.

It also helps them develop mindfulness skills, improve impulse control, decrease behavioral outbursts, and improve social interactions (Chen et al., 2013; Losinski, Sanders, and Wiseman, 2016).

Benefits of Sensory Play

Sensory play exposes children to new experiences that, in turn, might trigger new emotions. They then have opportunities to learn to recognize and deal with these big emotions. For example, when children experience displeasure at the sight of certain textures (think lumpy or slimy) or disgust at a pungent odor, they learn to recognize the emotion. With help from a caregiver, they can correctly label that emotion and use self-regulation skills to manage their reactions to the displeasing sensations. Well-regulated children will be able to transfer this skill to other aspects of their day when they encounter similar situations. This doesn't happen overnight, but with practice and repeated exposure to sensory play, children will develop a repertoire of familiar emotions and remain calm and in control of their thoughts and feelings in many situations they encounter during the school day.

When children enjoy, or at the very least tolerate, sensory play, they are more likely to develop a tolerance to many types of sensory input. For example, those who can play with slime in a sensory bin or use fingerpaint are more likely to remain calm and in control of their emotions when pudding, ketchup, or oatmeal accidentally gets on their hands or clothing during mealtime. What might have triggered a meltdown for a child with few sensory play experiences needs little more than a quick handwashing for a well-regulated child who regularly engages in sensory play and is comfortable with a slimy or lumpy texture.

Beyond touch, sensory play can include smell, taste, sight, and movement, and can be incorporated into established classroom routines. Sensory inputs can be used to both calm children and get their attention as they participate in circle time and centers, transition between activities, have meals and snacks, and play outside.

Types of Sensory Play

There are five main types of sensory play to incorporate into the school day to help children develop strong self-regulation skills:

- Tactile or messy play
- Visual play
- Auditory play
- Movement
- Proprioception

Tactile or Messy Play

Tactile or messy play is one of the main types of sensory play. When children play with a sensory bin, water table, or sandbox, they learn more than just how to tolerate being messy and dirty. Through open-ended messy play, children work on developing social skills, impulse control, and patience. Engaging in messy play supports children in developing patience, turn-taking, and the ability to listen to and follow rules. And remember, don't fear the mess! Cleanup should be part of the activity. When children clean up their messes, they learn important self-help, fine motor, and social skills.

One of the most common messy-play activities is the sensory bin—a box, bin, baking tray, or bowl filled with messy materials such as sand, water, slime, or shaving cream, along with manipulative items, that allows children to engage in open-ended sensory play contained to a specific space.

How to Make a Sensory Bin

To make a sensory bin, start with the container. Children may engage differently in sensory play based on the size and type of container. A large container will accommodate multiple children at one time and will encourage cooperative play. A small container, such as a baking sheet or bowl, will allow for individual and parallel play. As the educator, you have the ability to control the type of play you are interested in providing for your children simply by choosing the type of container. Consider containers such as the following.

- A sensory table for large classrooms so several children can play cooperatively
- A plastic bin with a lid; under-the-bed totes with wheels work great
- Baking sheets or bowls
- Muffin tins

Next, add the base material, which can be dry or wet. A wet base is messy and may stick to the child's clothing, skin, and any items you add to the bin. Examples include water, water beads, shaving cream, slime, or playdough. A dry base is messy but will not stick to the child's clothing, skin, or the items you add to the bin. Examples include packaging peanuts, shredded paper, yarn, pompoms, sand, kinetic sand, or a sand substitute such as Kidfetti.

Then, choose the add-ins. At this stage, you can think about what you want your children to learn while playing in the sensory bin. For example, you can add items that match the theme of a lesson, such as ocean animals or forests. You can add letters or numbers to promote letter- and number-recognition skills. Hide puzzle pieces and encourage children to find them and put the puzzle together. Spoons, tongs, measuring cups, sieves, and bowls can support fine motor and self-help skills.

How to Make a Sensory Bag

Tactile sensory play can also occur beyond the bin. For example, children may engage in non-messy sensory play with sensory bags. A sensory bag is similar to a sensory bin in that it has a base and specific add-ins such as animals or letters, and the activity is contained. However, using a container such as ziplock bag, pencil pouch, or other closed, see-through item allows a child to play without getting messy.

To make a sensory bag, start with the container. Use a small, sealable plastic bag; a one-gallon, sealable plastic freezer bag; or a soft, see-through pencil case.

Next, add the base, which can be wet or dry. Wet bases include oil and water, paint, shaving cream, slime, and hair gel. Dry bases include sand, sand substitutes, or small pebbles.

Then, choose the add-ins. You can use items that match the theme of the lesson, letters or numbers, glitter, and paint. Seal the bag with clear packing tape to make sure it doesn't tear.

Visual Sensory Play

Visual sensory play is typically used to calm children who are feeling overwhelmed or dysregulated. Visual sensory toys such as sand timers, glitter jars, liquid motion toys, and sensory tubes provide repetitive, soothing input that can help children who are feeling upset, allowing them to regroup, calm down, and focus on what they need to.

The gentle, flowing movement inherent in visual sensory toys is an important tool in early-learning classrooms, as it provides children with an opportunity to engage in purposeful play that is calming. Children who are experiencing a big emotion may be unable to calm down on their own. Engaging in soothing visual sensory play can help them shift their focus from the big emotion they are feeling to the soothing movement.

How to Make a Glitter Jar

A glitter jar is a type of sensory tube, but the add-ins are limited to glitter and possibly paint or food coloring. Start with the container. Glitter jars can be made with plastic water bottles or any clear plastic container that has a sealable lid.

Add the base. The thicker the base, the more slowly the glitter will move through it. Combine water or rubbing alcohol with oil, glue, or hair gel. This way, the liquids will not blend together, creating the desired visual effect. Thin bases include water, rubbing alcohol, and baby oil. Thick bases include hair gel, vegetable oil, and clear glue. You can also add shampoo or liquid soap (do not combine these with water).

Next, choose the add-ins, such as glitter and food coloring, watercolor, or acrylic paint.

Finally, seal the container with hot glue or duct tape.

How to Make a Sensory Tube

Like a glitter jar, a sensory tube is an inexpensive visual sensory toy filled with gently moving, colorful objects. When children are overwhelmed, engaging with a sensory tube is an excellent way to help them shift their focus away from the big feeling to calm down and regain control of their emotions. Sensory tubes also help with visual focus and attention.

Start with the container. Sensory tubes can be made with plastic water bottles or any clear plastic container that has a sealable lid.

Add the base, which can be thin for quicker movement or thick for slower movement. Thin bases include water, rubbing alcohol, and baby oil. Thick bases include hair gel, vegetable oil, clear glue, shampoo, and liquid soap. (Do not combine shampoo or soap with water.)

Add water or rubbing alcohol to create a visual separation.

Next, choose the add-ins, such as glitter, sequins, and beads, as well as food coloring, watercolor, or acrylic paint. Seal the container with hot glue or duct tape.

Visual Sensory Play to Encourage Seated Attention

Seated activities require extra focus that is hard for many young children to sustain. When children lack the ability to sit and focus for an age-appropriate amount of time, they may exhibit challenging behaviors. Sensory play activities that require a strong visual focus, such as I Spy, sorting treasure hunts, and look-and-find books, can help children focus and sustain their attention and offer opportunities for children to practice patience and perseverance. These activities are both open-ended and structured, providing highly stimulating engagement that children have control over, but there is no order or need to find all of the hidden objects.

How to Make an I Spy Bottle or Bag

An I Spy bottle is easy to make and encourages visual focus, sustained attention, and the ability to stay seated and engaged in one activity for an age-appropriate amount of time. Rather than just asking children to find objects in a book or on a piece of paper, I Spy bottles require them to shake, turn, and physically interact with the bottle. This added sensory requirement helps increase attention and focus.

Start with the container. Use a plastic water bottle or any clear plastic container that has a sealable lid. If you are making an I Spy bag, use a heavy-duty one-gallon freezer bag, double-bagged.

Next, add the base. It should be dry and move easily in the container. Do not overfill the container with the base material or it will be difficult to find the add-in items. Fill the container two-thirds full with colored sand, shredded paper, small beads, birdseed, or kinetic sand.

Choose the add-ins. They may be themed, such as animals, letters, numbers, and so on, or may simply be interesting items to look at. Do not overfill the container; add enough materials that it all moves freely and children can spy what they are searching for easily.

On a piece of card stock or an index card, create a visual key so children know what they are looking for. Laminate the key for durability.

Finally, seal the bottle with superglue, hot glue, or duct tape. Seal the I Spy bag with duct tape.

Auditory Sensory Inputs and Play

Auditory sensory inputs help set the mood and tone of the classroom. A loud classroom with poor acoustics might make children feel overly excited and overstimulated. Their voice levels will increase to match the decibel level of the classroom. A quiet classroom with calm music encourages the children to remain calm and in control of their emotions and actions.

Music can soothe children during challenging parts of the day. Slow, rhythmic music played when children enter the classroom in the morning, during meals, and during rest times may help children regulate their nervous systems to better handle their emotions.

In play, exploring the different sounds objects make, and talking about qualities such as quiet versus loud, will cultivate problem-solving skills, and attention and focus. Children will learn to listen and pay attention to sounds and build an understanding of sound qualities, such as loud versus soft sounds, high-pitched versus low-pitched sounds, and fast versus slow.

When children understand the qualities of sound, especially quiet versus loud sounds, they can transfer this knowledge to their own voices. By experiencing loud and soft sounds during sensory play, children learn the difference between the two. Discussing the qualities of loud and soft sounds helps children learn that a sound that is too loud can be disruptive to others and a sound that is too quiet is ineffective and hard to hear. This knowledge can encourage children who speak softly to speak louder and those who are too loud to quiet their voices. Sound tubes are a great way for children to explore sounds in their play.

How to Make a Sound Tube

A sound tube filled with quiet items will produce a quiet sound, which will sound the same no matter how vigorously it is shaken. A sound tube filled with loud items will produce a loud sound and will produce different sounds depending on how it is shaken. Explore this phenomenon with children, helping them identify when and why the sounds are different.

Start with the container. A sound tube can be made with plastic water bottles or any clear plastic container that has a sealable lid.

Add the base material, such as sand, being careful not to overfill the container.

Next, choose the add-ins. They can be quiet items or ones that will produce a louder sound. Quiet items include cotton balls, pompoms, feathers, and sequins. Loud items include small bells and pebbles or fish-tank rocks.

Finally, seal the jar with superglue, hot glue, or duct tape.

Movement Sensory Play

Movement activities involving children's balance, coordination, and sense of space can help them remain alert and calm throughout the school day. Sensory play that involves movement is a preventative type of input. Activities such as dancing, walking on a balance bar or tape on the floor, obstacle courses, and swinging improve gross-motor coordination, cooperation with peers, and listening skills. For those children who are fidgeters and wigglers, consistently moving their bodies throughout the day helps them sit longer and focus on what they are learning. When the school day is filled with regular opportunities for children to exercise and move their bodies, they will be better prepared to learn and retain the information they are learning. The movements will also decrease disruptive and challenging behaviors.

Some young children struggle to remain seated and attentive to an activity for an age-appropriate amount of time. This type of behavior is disruptive to the whole classroom. Children who crave movement input but don't get enough of it tend to have difficulty staying seated and attending to the task at hand for an age-appropriate amount of time. They may intentionally fall out of their chairs, refuse to stay seated, or fidget in their seats. And when they are working hard just to sit still, they have little attentional capacity left to focus on learning activities.

By engaging in regular sensory play that involves movement, they are often able to "store up" that input and access it later during seated activities. Providing opportunities to move, work on balance, or hold yoga poses between times during the day when children are seated will help them sit for longer periods and concentrate on what they are supposed to. Consider providing opportunities for movement in two- to ten-minute intervals each hour throughout the day—but especially before circle time, mealtimes, and seated work.

Simple Movement Games That Encourage Attention and Focus

Games such as the following are easy to play in most classrooms or playgrounds as they require few or no materials:

- Freeze Dance
- Duck, Duck, Goose
- What Time Is It, Mr. Fox?
- Red Light, Green Light
- Scavenger hunts

A number of online resources, such as GoNoodle (https://www.gonoodle.com/), Move to Learn (http://movetolearnms.org/), and Koo Koo Kanga Roo (https://www.youtube.com/KooKooKangaRoo), offer guided movement. These sites offer free streaming child-friendly songs and lyrics with dancers that children can follow. Each song is two to three minutes long, an ideal length for a movement break. Several songs can be used to provide a longer time for movement play.

How to Make an Obstacle Course around the Classroom

Creating an obstacle course in the classroom is a fun and easy way to provide children with movement opportunities while encouraging attention and focus. Obstacle courses do not need to be made of expensive items. Make sure there is enough space for children to move safely through the obstacle course you will create. The purpose is for children to crawl, jump, walk, and move their bodies. Design a three- to five-step obstacle course by placing objects from the classroom in the open space. For example:

- Place a line of masking tape on the floor for children to walk along.
- Place a cushion on the floor for children to jump over.
- Place a chair for children to walk around.

Demonstrate or describe the steps to the course so the children will know what to do. For added fun, encourage the children to imagine they are an animal or an explorer traveling through a jungle.

Follow the Leader

Similar to an obstacle course, this game provides children with movement input while encouraging attention and focus. This is a great game to play outdoors during recess with children who struggle to fill their outdoor time productively. Give the class directions. Let them know that you are the leader and their job is to follow your every move around the outdoor space: walk in silly ways, jump, turn in a circle, and so on.

Literacy Scavenger Hunt

Working on literacy skills while engaging in a scavenger hunt around the classroom is a fun way for children to move their bodies while learning. In pairs or on their own, children can search the classroom for sight words, objects around the room that begin with particular letters, or rhyming words. Decide on the type of scavenger hunt the children will engage in, aligning it with the classroom's current literacy goals.

Develop the scavenger hunt using pictures, easy words, or free online printables. Give the class directions, reminding them of the classroom rules they should follow. Set a time limit and tell them to start their scavenger hunt. Give assistance as needed and encourage problem-solving skills. As time winds down, give a five-minute warning and a one-minute warning to support time management. Bring the class back together and go over the scavenger-hunt results.

Balance Activities to Support Seated Attention

Sitting on the floor during circle time, upright in a chair during mealtime, or at a desk to focus on work requires a lot of balance. Children who struggle with balance may seek movement to help keep themselves upright and engaged.

There are movement activities children can do while seated, called passive movement inputs, which can help them focus and improve their balance. These options include sitting on an exercise ball instead of in a regular chair, placing an inflatable cushion on a school chair, T-stools, and sitting on an oversized pillow during circle time.

Standing balance activities, such as the following, help improve children's core muscles, which will support sustained attention during seated activities.

- Walking along a masking-tape "balance beam"
- Hopscotch
- Games in which children practice standing on one foot, then the other, then with their eyes closed
- Yoga poses

The Inspired Treehouse website offers a list of fun ways to encourage children to balance on one foot. You can find it here: https://theinspiredtreehouse.com/20-creative-ways-practice-single-leg-stance/

How to Make a Masking-Tape Balance Beam

Masking tape can be used to create balance beams, obstacle courses, and hopscotch paths, which help children safely work on balance and core strength. To begin, simply adhere masking tape to the floor in a long, straight line. Encourage children to walk along the line without falling off.

Once they are skilled at walking along a straight line, create a zigzag or curved line for them to walk along. Then, add obstacles such as cushions to the line, and challenge the children to jump or step over them.

Proprioception: Deep Pressure and Heavy Work Activities

Proprioception is how the body senses movement and understands how to move through space. It is responsible for our ability to kick a ball without falling over, walk through a crowded environment without bumping into things, and plan our motor actions for success.

There are two types of proprioception activities: those that apply deep pressure to the muscles and joints and those that involve heavy muscle work. Play and activities that involve deep pressure create tension within the body. They involve pushing, pulling, and carrying heavy objects. They offer the body extra sensory input and help children stay alert and calm. Deep pressure and heavy muscle work activities include the following:

- Yoga
- Jumping on a trampoline
- Bouncing on a therapy ball
- Animal-walking around the classroom or the playground
- Holding a plank position
- Wall pushups
- Blowing bubbles
- Chewing gum
- Raking, sweeping, or vacuuming

Deep pressure input and heavy muscle work activities encourage self-regulation skills and help children feel alert and calm. Engaging in heavy work or play for just five to fifteen minutes can improve children's focus for up to two hours (Ayres, 1972). Activities such as swinging on the playground, practicing yoga poses, completing obstacle courses, dancing, and playing Freeze Tag can ensure that children are better able to sit and focus during circle time, at centers, and at mealtimes.

Chapter 4:

The Self-Regulated Preschool or Pre-K Classroom

Designing a sensory-rich classroom environment requires intentional thought and planning by the teacher. The effort will pay off in helping preschool and prekindergarten children remain calm and in control of their emotions throughout the school day.

The Physical Environment

First, consider the physical environment itself. It's not possible to change the size, shape, and natural lighting options. But with careful consideration, it is possible to make the most out of the space and lighting by placing furniture consistently, creating open space so children can move around the classroom safely and without bumping into others, offering visual and auditory supports to help children remember classroom rules and routines, reducing visual and auditory distractions, and keeping natural light sources free from obstruction.

Furniture Arrangement

The way furniture is arranged in the classroom can maximize space, separate the room into different learning areas, and enhance the classroom layout. In fact, the furniture and how it is placed provide the primary structure of the classroom. This structure helps give children a sense of security as they independently navigate the room and the materials within it. When children feel knowledgeable and in control of their environment, they are better able to remain calm and in control of their emotions.

With careful consideration of the number of children in the classroom, the size of the room, and permanent fixtures such as doors, windows, closets, and sinks, design the classroom in such a way that furniture defines areas of the room. These areas might include a cozy corner, library area, pretend play area, and seated learning areas.

Visual Supports

Visual supports help children with time management and support self-regulation. Young children do not have a good sense of time. Using visual supports in the classroom will help them visualize how long they have to wait until it is their turn or when it will be time to go outside or eat lunch.

Common visual supports include a visual timer, a visual schedule, and a sign-up system for centers.

To help children begin to grasp how time passes, a visual timer is a great aid. A visual timer may be a sand timer or one that mimics a clock face: a colored disc appears as the desired time is dialed on the timer. As time passes, the color disappears. When the time is up, all the color has disappeared. This type of visual support shows children how long they have to wait and also assures them that their turn is coming up soon. Visual timers may also be used to show children how much time remains for a given turn or activity to help them independently manage their workload and motivate them to stay on task.

A visual schedule, a combination of pictures and words that shows children the schedule for the day, should be placed in an easy-to-view spot so children may reference it often. This helps them know when free time, recess, and mealtimes are so that they can independently manage their time, hunger, and patience.

Center time is often a difficult part of the school day. Implementing a visual sign-up system is a great way to help children regulate their emotions when the area they want to play in is full. A sign-up system allows children to see which center activities are full or have room for more children. Older children may sign in to a center using a laminated card with their name on it. For children who are preliterate, laminated cards with both a photo of the child and their name is a great visual aid. Children may Velcro their card to a center sign-in sheet, or they can place their card in a pocket chart specific to each center.

Additional visual supports that help support independence and self-regulation skills include the following:

- An attendance pocket chart that shows who is at school today
- Taping laminated photos or names of each student to a specific spot at the learning tables or on the carpet for circle time so that each student has a defined personal space they know to go to
- A visual schedule comprised of pictures, a time frame, and words highlighting the classroom routine to remind children of the order of the daily schedule and to help them recognize where they should be, when they should be there, and what happens next
- Visuals, such as shapes, numbers, boxes, or footprints taped to the floor 12–24 inches apart, to help children line up when transitioning out of the classroom. Knowing where to line up while respecting personal space helps children remain in control of their bodies and emotions while transitioning out of the classroom.

Auditory Supports

When used intentionally, auditory signals and reminders support rule-following and transitions and help promote seamless classroom management. For example, transition songs such as "Clean up, clean up, everybody everywhere. Clean up, clean up, everybody do their share" signal to children that it is time to clean up before moving on to another activity.

Clapping can be used as a signal that the children should pause what they are doing and listen to the teacher. The teacher initiates a clapping pattern, and the children copy it. Then, they turn their attention to the teacher. Short chants, such as "Now it's time to listen . . . listen . . . listen . . . listen," also work well as signals.

These songs, chants, and clapping patterns support classroom management because they help children know that a transition is about to happen; remember classroom routines, such as the steps for handwashing; refocus when the class becomes rowdy; and listen and pay attention.

Reducing Distractions

To further support children's ability to focus on what they should, consider limiting unnecessary visual and auditory distractions. To reduce visual distractions, consider providing closed storage for toys, games, and items not in continual use. Decrease clutter and avoid filling the walls with too many posters and projects.

Auditory distractions are sounds that affect a child's ability to listen and pay attention to what they are supposed to. This could be a noisy hallway, outdoor sounds coming from an open window, a loud heater, or even the ticking of a clock. To reduce unnecessary auditory distractions, play quiet, rhythmic music or white noise in the background. Try to design the classroom in a way that seated learning centers are far away from the door. A neat and uncluttered classroom that has few extraneous sounds and is easy to move around will support every child's ability to remain focused.

Lighting

Proper lighting affects children's ability to see what they are working with and influences energy levels, focus, and attention. Studies show that a combination of natural and artificial light (lamps, overhead lighting, and so on) helps improve focus, attention, and motivation (Boyce, et al., 2006; Smolders and de Kort, 2013). When possible, replace overhead fluorescent lights with LED bulbs. Fluorescent bulbs have been found to emit a harsh light that causes fatigue, loss of focus, and eye strain in many people. Maximize natural light sources as much as possible and consider placing learning centers in a space where there is a lot of natural light.

Sensory Spaces

Next, consider designating specific sensory spaces within the classroom. The most common include a calm-down area, a movement space, and a tactile space. These spaces provide children with safe, inviting sensory experiences that can help them calm down when they feel frustrated or overwhelmed, engage in movement to help their attention and focus, or stimulate their creative side while working on problem-solving skills in the tactile area. Each of these spaces should be center-time options.

Serene Sensory Space

A serene sensory space is a part of the classroom where children may go to calm down when they become upset or overwhelmed. This space can be called the quiet corner, calm-down corner, or something similar. All children should be encouraged to use it so they can learn to pause, think, and then react. It will also help them calm down when they've become angry or frustrated and are struggling to regulate themselves to calm down. This safe and cozy space shouldn't be used for punishments or time-outs, but as a place to enter for a few minutes when self-regulation is hard to accomplish. Introduce this space the same way other learning centers are introduced to the class.

When creating a calming space in the classroom, start with comfortable seating options such as beanbag chairs, oversized pillows, floor cushions, or gym mats. Include calming sensory inputs such as visual soothers, sand timers, I Spy tubes, a kaleidoscope, and books to look through.

Also include tactile objects such as fidget toys (that should remain in the sensory space); weighted stuffies for deep pressure input; fabrics with interesting textures such as scarves, silk, and faux fur; contained sensory bags; and fluffy pillows. For calming movement, add a rocking chair or rocking horse.

Children will need to be taught how to use this space. Explain how to transition to the space without disrupting the rest of the class, how long they may remain in the space, how many children may be in the space at one time, and how to use the items in the space.

Louie becomes so angry at times that it's hard for him to calm down on his own. He cries and throws what he is working on. Recently, Ms. Steph, Louie's teacher, has been working with the whole class to remind them that the cozy corner is a place children may visit when they feel overwhelmed and need time to calm down. During circle time, she reads books that talk about big feelings. She brings items from the cozy corner such as the fidget toys, sand timers, and sensory tubes to circle time and allows the children to interact with everything while she reminds them how to use the items. She offers herself as an example, saying, "When I feel angry, I like to squeeze this stress ball." She squeezes the stress ball as hard as she can. "When I feel frustrated, I like to look at this sensory tube," she continues, shaking it a bit. "I like the way the glitter swirls around and makes pretty patterns." She then opens the discussion to the group by asking, "What do you do when you feel angry or frustrated or sad?" After listening to the children's ideas, Ms. Steph finishes the lesson by asking the children to help her put the items back in the cozy corner. She gives them a quick tour of the space and reminds them that they may enter it when they need to. The next time Louie becomes angry, Ms. Steph approaches him calmly and says, "I see that you are feeling angry. Would you like to spend some time in the cozy corner? You'll find some things there that might help you calm down."

Movement Space

The purpose of a movement space is to allow children to safely receive movement input during the school day. Designating a movement space will give children the opportunity to engage in movement activities during the school day without a transition out of the classroom. This space should be designed to encourage children to dance, rock in a rocking chair, challenge their balance, or bounce on an exercise ball.

When children engage in movement before sustained sitting activities, they are better able to sit and pay attention, remaining calm and in control of their bodies and their behaviors. Allowing preschool and prekindergarten children the chance to engage in a few minutes of movement will support their ability to remain calm and in control for seated activities.

In this space, include items such as a rocking chair; an exercise ball placed in a plastic laundry basket, which allows children to bounce on the ball while it remains in one place; musical instruments to encourage shaking, clapping, tapping, and dancing; and a gym mat for yoga, jumping, and dancing.

Due to space limitations, a specific movement space may not be possible for all preschool classrooms. If this is the case, items for movement input, such as a child-sized rocking chair or small exercise ball placed in a plastic laundry basket, could be added to the serene sensory space. These dynamic seating options do not take up a lot of space but do allow children to get movement input in a safe yet effective way.

Tactile Space

A tactile space is an important part of a preschool or prekindergarten classroom because it provides children with sensory-rich opportunities to work on fine-motor skills, social skills, problem-solving, inhibitory control, and attentional flexibility. As they scoop, pour, dump, shake, and manipulate paintbrushes while playing in a cooperative and open-ended way, children are also developing these skills while having fun. They work on problem-solving skills as they explore sensory bins or sand and water tables. They engage with peers and learn to wait their turn, share limited resources, clean up messes, and navigate conflict.

Create a tactile space by adding opportunities for open-ended sensory play, such as sensory bins, tables, or troughs; a painting station; and a sand and water table.

Co-Regulation with Familiar Adults

Finally, consider the importance of co-regulation for this age group. Three- and four-year-olds are still learning how to regulate their reactions and will benefit from co-regulating with teachers during the school day. Encourage an environment where all children feel welcome, safe, and respected.

Talk about the classroom rules during circle time. Post visuals of the class schedule and rules in a spot where children can reference them easily. Celebrate the positive things children have done during morning or afternoon circle times and meetings. This reinforcement will help children develop a trusting relationship with their teacher so they will seek guidance when they struggle with self-regulation.

Simple and effective ways to support co-regulation with all children throughout the day include the following:

- Maintaining a consistent classroom routine
- Developing well-established classroom rules that are taught and talked about often
- Responding to all children according to their needs
- Fostering an environment in which all children feel safe and respected

Enrich the classroom with sensory play to support strong self-regulation skills for three- and four-year-olds and to help them remain calm and in control of their behaviors and emotions throughout the day. The following is an example of a sensory-rich preschool or prekindergarten day:

> As the children enter the classroom for morning drop-off, music is playing softly in the background. Each child is greeted warmly by a familiar caregiver and reminded of the drop-off routine: sign in, take off your coat and hang it and your backpack in your cubby, then choose a center to explore.
>
> Free-play sensory opportunities include the tactile space with its sensory bins and sand and water play; the visual space with its liquid motion toys, sand timer, and I Spy sensory tubes; the movement space where children can engage in yoga or freeze dance. In the block center, children can push toy trains, cars, and trucks along a track or build with the blocks.
>
> When it is time to gather for morning circle, the teacher signals the class to transition with a sound or clap. The music has been turned off so the children can focus on listening to the teacher.

Few visual distractions exist in the background so the class can visually focus on the teacher. During circle time, children who fidget may sit on a cushion or pillow for movement input and also to remind them where their spot is. The circle-time activities are interactive and engaging and designed to last for fifteen minutes or so. The children actively participate in all activities instead of passively listening.

During free play/center time, the children understand what centers are available and how many children may be in a center at one time. They know that if their preferred center is full, they may play in another center until a spot opens up. They engage in sensory opportunities such as sensory bins supporting the theme of the day or week in the tactile space and fingerpainting in the art center. The visual space, with its liquid motion toys, sand timer, I Spy sensory tubes, and other items is a popular center. Some children enjoy pushing toy cars around a track or building a block tower. The dramatic play area is always full, as the children love to dress up and engage in pretend play.

During snack and mealtimes, quiet music plays in the background. The teacher sings or chants to remind the children to wash their hands and then sit down to eat. To encourage socialization among children, the area near the tables has few visual and auditory distractions. As they eat, towels and water are available for children who don't like getting their hands messy. Passive movement options, such as T-stools and chair cushions, are also available for children who fidget in their seats. When it is time to clean up, the teacher sings a song or chants to help children remember the routine.

The children head outdoors to play. The teacher encourages movement on the playground structures as well as running, skipping, jumping, and other physical activities. Children can also choose to engage in messy play in the sandbox or sand and water table.

When it is time to head back indoors for rest time, the teacher signals the transition with a chant. In the classroom, white or brown noise plays to muffle extraneous sounds, and a diffuser lightly scents the air with vanilla or lavender. The room is dimly lit with minimal natural light sources. Few visual distractions on the walls help the children calm down and relax.

Afternoon circle time proceeds similarly to the morning circle time. Afterward, children engage in center time and sensory opportunities.

Chapter 5:

The Self-Regulated Kindergarten Classroom

Self-regulation and executive function skills should be supported in the kindergarten classroom as children become more independent and will rely on these cognitive skills to remain well regulated throughout the day. On average, kindergartners spend more time seated and engaged in curriculum-based learning than they did in preschool and prekindergarten. The school day is more structured, and rest time is shortened considerably, if it happens at all.

Develop Classroom Rules to Support Self-Regulation

Creating a classroom environment that supports executive function and self-regulation requires foresight, planning, and time. Much of this revolves around the classroom rules and routines. Including children in the development of visual supports will demonstrate the importance of the class rules, helping the children feel invested and more likely to follow the rules. Discuss the class rules using positive language and display them throughout the classroom.

Keep the rules simple, using as few words as possible. For example, when children are creating the classroom rules, they may start with "Don't be mean." With guidance from the teacher, this statement can transform into one or two rules, such as "Be kind" or "Play nice." A suggestion such as, "Don't interrupt someone when they're talking," can be written as "Listen," or "Raise your hand."

Sensory Inputs to Support Self-Regulation and Executive Function Skills

Although there is less time for open-ended sensory play in many kindergarten classrooms, sensory input remains a valuable tool for supporting children as they learn and engage with their peers. Enhancing the classroom and learning activities with sensory opportunities stimulates the children's senses and improves their problem-solving, language development, social skills, and motor skills. Use sensory input to support children's self-regulation as they learn to manage their time, socialize with peers, transition from one activity to the next, and improve their literacy, math, science, and social studies skills.

Visual Inputs

Visual supports provide children with a sense of control over their day and help them stay calm and in control of their emotions. They also support children's patience, attentional flexibility, and inhibitory control. For example, a visual reminder of the classroom rules helps children remember what the rules are and supports them in respecting the rules. Tools to support time management and anticipate transitions, such as a visual schedule depicting the school day, remind them of the order of activities. A visual timer helps them understand how much time they have left to complete an activity. Other examples of visual supports for kindergarten classrooms include stickers on the floor showing where to line up and name tags at desks or tables reminding children where their seat is.

Teachers can model waiting, patience, and time management. For example, even though Jessie eats breakfast at school, during morning centers and circle time he often interrupts the class by saying, "I'm hungry." His teacher uses the visual schedule to help Jessie see when snack time is. "Right now it's free-choice time. Then, we have circle time. And then it's snack time." This visual support helps Jessie with self-control.

Sofia does not like to line up unless she gets to be first in line. When Mr. Matt, the class aide, asks her why, she tells him she doesn't want the other children to bump into her or touch her hair. At the end of the day, Mr. Matt decides to create a visual cue to help children respect one another's personal space while they line up to transition out of the classroom. He starts at the door and places stickers (masking tape works too) every fifteen to eighteen inches, one sticker for each child in the class. During morning meeting time, Mr. Matt introduces the class to the new visual support and explains how children should use the stickers to help them line up. Although he made this visual support with Sofia in mind, the stickers will benefit the whole class when they are transitioning out the door. They will help children maintain personal space and may diminish Sofia's desire to be first in line.

Auditory Inputs

Auditory supports also help with time management, working memory, and attentional inhibition. These include a timer and verbal warnings that let children know an activity is going to end. Teachers can use hand-clap patterns or chants such as, "One, two, three, eyes on me," to which children respond, "One, two, eyes on you." Drumbeats and chimes are auditory transition aids that help children feel in control of transitions without needing to be told by a teacher. Songs can describe an activity's routine, such as a cleanup song or a song about handwashing. When such tactics support children's executive function skills, they are better able to remain calm and in control of their actions and emotions.

Exploring the different sounds objects make and talking about those qualities, such as loud versus soft sounds, high-pitched versus low-pitched sounds, and fast versus slow sounds, will cultivate children's problem-solving skills, attention and focus, and learning how to listen and pay attention to sounds.

Exploring Sound with Sound Tubes

This is a fun activity that children may engage in during circle time or as a small-group exploration.

Intended outcomes:

- Engagement with learning opportunities through music
- Improved understanding and control of voice volume
- Improved problem-solving and fine-motor skill development

Materials:

Empty plastic containers with lids, such as empty playdough containers or empty water bottles

Plastic holiday eggs

Empty paper-towel tubes

Small rocks

Bells

Pompoms

Beads

Legos

Duct tape or hot glue (adult use only)

What to Do:

- First choose the container to serve as the tube. A clear container such as a water bottle will add a visual component. An opaque container will allow children to engage with the sound tube using only their auditory sense.
- Invite children to fill their sound tubes with different materials, encouraging them to think about the sound each might make.
- Once each tube has been filled with the desired material, seal it by folding and taping the ends of the paper towel roll or hot-gluing the lid.
- Students may make a variety of sound tubes, giving the class multiple opportunities to engage with the activity and learn about what sound is. Here are some suggestions:
    - Comparing sounds and describing the properties of sound (loud vs. soft, slow vs. fast)

- Matching similar sounds
- Guessing what type of sound a tube might make before shaking it
- Creating music as a group by shaking, rolling, or twisting the tubes all together

Movement Inputs

Kindergarten children benefit greatly from movement input during the school day. Although it may seem counterintuitive, the more children move their bodies throughout the day, the more able they are to attend to a seated activity. Many kindergarten schedules allow for only twenty minutes per day of recess. This is too little time for most children to get all the movement input their bodies need to stay alert and calm during the day. Adding movement opportunities to the regular school day and embedding movement opportunities into learning activities will support strong self-regulation skills. When movement is combined with learning, it also supports attentional flexibility, working memory, and inhibitory control, the executive functions children rely on to be successful in the classroom.

Literacy Scavenger Hunts

These activities combine movement and literacy learning to support targeted literacy skills. They also encourage social skills, problem solving, and active listening. Try them during small-group learning or literacy-center time.

Intended outcomes:

- Improved targeted literacy skills
- Improved attentional flexibility and working memory
- Social-skill development
- Improved problem-solving skills

Materials:

Card stock or index cards

Markers

What to Do:

- Sight-word scavenger hunt: Write common sight words on card stock, and place the cards around the classroom. Invite the children to search the classroom for the words and tell what they are when they find them.
- Rhyming-word scavenger hunt: Draw or print out pictures of objects and put them on card stock. For example, put a picture of a moon on a card. Ask children to find something that rhymes with *moon*, such as the word *June* on the calendar.
- Letter scavenger hunt: Give the children a list of the letters of the alphabet. Challenge them to find something in the classroom that begins with each letter sound.

Hopscotch through the Hallway

Transitions are an excellent time to provide children with extra movement input.

Intended outcomes:

- Structured movement input during hallway transitions
- Improved balance and core stability
- Improved working memory
- Practice with pattern recognition, counting, and number identification

Materials:

Painter's tape

What to Do:

- Using painter's tape, create a hopscotch design in a hallway. Tape a number from one to ten in each shape.
- Invite the children to hop or jump through the design when they transition as a class or any time they walk through the hallway on their own.
- Show them how to hop through the design following the pattern in sequential order.

Freeze Dance

A freeze dance is a great way to provide structured movement during whole-class activities, such as circle time. Try it when you have a little time available before a seated activity or any time when children are struggling to remain calm and in control of their bodies.

Intended outcomes:

- Improved attentional flexibility, working memory, and inhibitory control
- Improved attention and focus
- Improved core strength and balance

Materials:

Recorded music

What to Do:

- Ask the children to stand up and spread out a little so they do not run into each other.
- Tell them you will play music and they can dance any way they want to.
- When you stop the music, they have to freeze in place.
- When you restart the music, they can unfreeze and dance again.

Dance Along to Brain-Break Songs

This is another great way to provide structured movement during whole-class activities. Engaging in these goal-directed dancing activities will help reduce stress, frustration, and fidgeting and will improve attention, focus, core strength, and stability.

Intended outcomes:

- Learning and copying dance moves
- Improved attention and focus
- Improved core strength and balance
- Practice with pattern recognition

Materials:

Recorded music

What to Do:

- Make up dance movements with the children. For example, together come up with movements to do to "If You're Happy and You Know It." Alternatively, visit YouTube.com to find children's music and dance videos, such as Dr. Jean Feldman songs (https://www.youtube.com/user/drjeansongs) or Koo Koo Kanga Roo (https://www.youtube.com/KooKooKangaRoo).
- Play the music and encourage the children to do the dance.

Tactile Inputs

While there may not be time for kindergartners to engage in as much open-ended sensory play as they did in preschool and prekindergarten, these powerful sensory strategies can still be incorporated into the entire kindergarten day. Tactile inputs can promote self-regulation by:

- Soothing and calming children when they are not regulating their emotions well
- Engagement in activities
- Improved small-motor skills
- Improved problem-solving and attentional flexibility skills
- Improved attention and focus

Serene Sensory Space

Kindergartners will benefit from a serene sensory space in the classroom that allows them to calm down and work on self-regulation when their emotions get the better of them. When children feel angry, anxious, or overwhelmed and have difficulty calming down to focus on their schoolwork, allowing them to spend time in a calm space will help reset their emotions and get their regulation under control. This is not a time-out area; it is a positive or neutral place to visit. It's a place where children can spend five to ten minutes processing their emotions and calming down so they can return to learning with the class in control of their feelings and actions. Make sure the seating is comfortable. Include books, fidgets that remain in this space, visual soothers, and sensory bags, soft fabrics, and sensory jars. This is a safe space to go to without being removed from the classroom, allowing the teacher to continue teaching the rest of the class. It minimizes disruptions and respects the needs of all children.

Introduce the space and show the class how to use it. Be sure to do this before children struggle with self-regulation so they don't feel like they are being punished. Children who are unaware that they are not regulating their emotions may need the teacher to encourage them to go to and use the calm space.

Tactile Input to Enhance Attention and Focus

Adding tactile input to traditional kindergarten activities is a great way to keep children interested in what they are learning. Instead of working on letter formation and number sense on a computer screen or a pencil-and-paper activity, use playdough or putty to work on letter formation or pompoms to work on counting skills. Children can also practice simple addition and subtraction with counting cubes or practice writing in shaving cream or colored sand.

Tactile Input to Improve Fine-Motor Skills

Play and learning opportunities with an emphasis on tactile input helps children improve hand strength and fine-motor skills in a fun and engaging way. When children scoop, pour, dump, and dig in sensory bins, they practice motor skills they need to feed themselves neatly, write, color, and draw. Kindergartners with strong hand muscles and good fine-motor skills have a solid foundation for remaining calm and in control of their emotions when they learn new skills.

Sensory-Rich Kindergarten Classroom That Supports Self-Regulation

Enrich the classroom with sensory play to support strong self-regulation skills for five-year-olds and to help them remain calm and in control of their behaviors and emotions throughout the day. The following is an example of a sensory-rich kindergarten day:

> As the children enter the classroom in the morning, music is playing softly in the background. Each child is greeted warmly by their teacher and reminded of the routine: sign in, take off your coat and hang it and your backpack in your cubby, then choose a center to explore.
>
> When it is time to gather for morning circle, the teacher signals the class to transition with a sound or clap. The music has been turned off so the children can focus on listening to the teacher. Few visual distractions exist in the background so the class can visually focus on the teacher. During circle time, children who fidget may sit on a cushion or pillow for movement input and also to remind them where their spot is. The circle-time activities are interactive and engaging and designed to last for fifteen minutes or so. The children actively participate in all activities instead of passively listening.
>
> During free play/center time, the children understand what centers are available and how many children may be in a center at one time. They know that, if their preferred center is full, they may play in another center until a spot opens up. Some children enjoy pushing toy cars around a track or building a block tower. The dramatic play area is always full, as the children love to dress up and engage in pretend play. They have access to a sensory space, where they can explore sensory bins and materials. In the movement area, they may rock in a rocking chair or bounce on an exercise ball. They know the calming space is always available if they need it.
>
> In the library area, they may look at favorite books or listen to a recording of a book being read as they follow along. The

children's names and the alphabet are visible for reference. They have easy access to paper and pencils, crayons, colored pencils, and markers. In a project-based center, a visual model of the completed project might be available. As they complete work or have questions, their teacher is available to talk with them.

During snack and mealtimes, if the children eat in the classroom, quiet music plays in the background. The teacher sings or chants to remind the children to wash their hands and then sit down to eat. The area near the tables has limited visual and auditory distractions, to encourage socialization among children. As they eat, towels and water are available for children who don't like getting their hands messy. Passive movement options, such as T-stools and chair cushions, are also available for children who fidget in their seats. When it is time to clean up, the teacher sings a song or chants to help children remember the routine.

The children head outdoors to play. The teacher encourages movement on the playground structures as well as running, skipping, jumping, and other physical activities. The teacher offers structured movement such as Follow the Leader and outdoor scavenger hunts. Children can also choose to engage in messy play in the sandbox.

When it is time to head back indoors for afternoon learning activities, the teacher signals the transition with a chant.

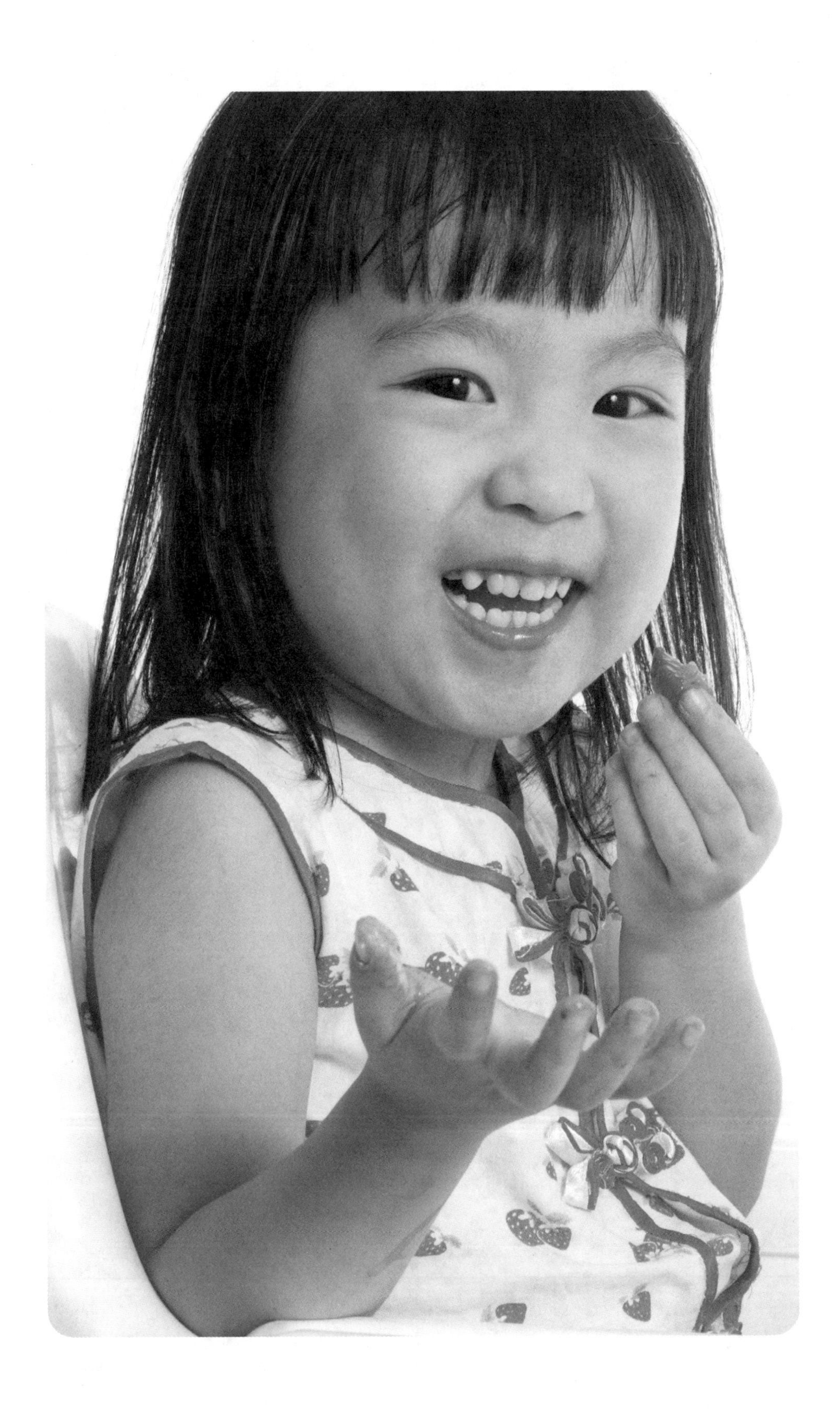

Chapter 6:
Calm during Mealtimes

Mealtime is an important school-day activity. It is an ideal time to encourage communication, work on self-help skills, and foster social skills, all of which require a great deal of self-regulation. To support every student in the classroom, consider working on emotional regulation, problem solving, self-help skills, and social skills through sensory play activities before snacks and meals. Because mealtime happens at about the same time each day, teachers and caregivers have the opportunity to lay some groundwork for practicing self-regulation skills during centers, at circle time, and during outside recess.

The Sensory Qualities of Foods

The look, feel, smell, taste, and temperature of foods matter a great deal to young children. Adults have had decades to become accustomed to various foods. They are able to regulate and stay calm when exposed to foods they dislike. However, many young children have not had enough experience with foods and flavors to develop these skills.

During a snack or meal, caregivers should take into consideration the foods' sensory components. What does the food look like? Is it presented in a visually pleasing way? Many young children dislike foods that are runny, stringy, lumpy, or slimy, not because of the taste, but simply because the food looks displeasing to them. What is the texture?

Crunchy and smooth textures are usually the easiest for children to tolerate. Foods that have mixed textures, such as soups, chili, oatmeal, rice, or tapioca pudding, tend to be the ones children dislike.

Consider the temperature of the food. Most young children prefer foods that are not too cold or too hot. And finally, consider the scent. How does the room smell? Is one food or meal overpowering everything else? Most young children have a strong sense of smell, so foods with a powerful odor might overwhelm them and cause them to lose their appetites.

From birth through age six, mealtimes provide novel sensory experiences and require processing sensory input from various foods. Many children display picky eating because they interpret these novel tastes, textures, and smells as displeasure. Hesitation to try new foods is common among young children. It can take up to twenty tries before they decide that they like it. Seeing other children and adults try the food can be helpful, as can getting the chance to say, "No, thank you," and to try again on another day. Fostering a nurturing environment, while supporting their sensory systems early in the day, helps children demonstrate good self-regulation skills when they are presented with foods that they dislike.

Sensory Play and Activities to Support Self-Regulation during Mealtime

During meals and snacks, young children will get messy, interact with new foods and textures they may not like, and sit at the table for the duration of the meal. They will also work on their communication and social skills, sharing limited resources, taking turns, and practicing their manners. The following sensory strategies will support each of these self-regulation skills.

Picky Eaters

Often, children present as picky eaters because of how a food looks and or feels in their mouths. Messy play with nonfood items that have varying textures encourages exploration and self-control in a fun and less stressful way. When children develop strategies to tolerate messy play, they learn to regulate their emotions while they engage with textures they dislike. This lays a strong foundation for self-regulation skills that will translate to mealtime, giving them the tools to stay calm and in control of their emotions even when they see or feel a food with a displeasing texture.

Engaging in messy tactile play will also teach them how to avoid displeasing textures in a socially appropriate way. This type of exploration empowers them to say no to interacting with the textures while maintaining control of their emotions. A caregiver can help them with appropriate language to use, suggesting, for example, "No, I don't want to play with this. I don't like the way it looks and feels." Or "No, thank you. I don't want to play with this. I will play with something else."

With support and reminders, children can use these same statements when presented with foods they dislike. And they can do so without fussing, crying, or having a tantrum. They will maintain control of their emotions and eat the other foods on their plate. Of course, if children also decide to eat a previously undesirable food, that is a bonus. Self-regulation is the goal, and we can teach it through sensory play.

Sensory Bin

Expose children to a wide variety of messy textures so they can learn to self-regulate when they interact with something they dislike. Engaging in play in a sensory bin is a great way to encourage self-regulation for children who struggle with different food textures.

Intended outcomes:

- Learning to tolerate the look and feel of a variety of textures
- Learning to manage emotions without becoming overly upset or angry when their hands or clothing get messy
- Developing strategies to remain calm when they engage in messy play, which transfer to snack and mealtime

Materials:

Plastic bin

Water beads

Water

Kinetic sand

Inexpensive shampoo

Colored body wash

Plastic food items

Themed items that match the season or a holiday

Toy dinosaurs, land and ocean animals, construction toys

Paper towels or cloth

What to Do:

- Add the materials to the sensory bin. Choose a wet base, such as water beads, or a combination of wet and dry bases, such as water with kinetic sand. Then, choose highly desirable add-ins, which may help resistant children play in the bin even if they dislike the look of the base material. **Note:** Using shampoo and body wash as the base will be very messy. However, children who dislike getting their hands messy may not mind trying to engage with this bin if they know it is soap rather than just a sticky, slimy input.
- Have the sensory bin available during center/free-choice time, and encourage children to play while you are close by. Adults can support this behavior by having paper towels or a cloth on hand.
- If children engage in the sensory bin and have a negative reaction to the feeling, the adult can help them stay calm, wash their hands, and move on to a different activity. This is self-regulation! Praise children for their bravery and tell them what you observed: "I saw you play with that gooey stuff. You did such a good job of not getting upset when it stuck to your hands. You cleaned it off, and now it's all gone. I'm proud of you."
- Later, during snack and mealtime, the adult can remind the children how brave and mature they were, hoping that if they encounter foods they dislike, they will remain well regulated by using the skills they just learned by playing in the sensory bin.

- **Important to note:** Some children will refuse to engage in the sensory bin. This is okay. Being around the sensory bin gives them the opportunity to look at the texture. They can still learn to tolerate it and develop strong social skills and empowered language to use during mealtime.

Sensory Bag

Different from a sensory bin, a sensory bag allows children to engage in a tactile activity in parallel with one another. Seated together during circle time or in small groups at their tables, children can play with sensory bags, interacting with the texture of the base while observing the bag's contents without actually getting messy.

Intended outcomes:

- Developing the ability to tolerate the look and feel of a variety of textures
- Learning to manage emotions at the sight and feeling of different textures
- Developing strategies to remain calm at the sight of a messy texture

Materials:

Gallon-size ziplock bags

Baby oil or vegetable oil

Water

Paint

Glitter

Hair gel

Pompoms in various sizes

Packing tape

What to Do:

- An ideal sensory bag for a picky eater is one that has a base with various textures and is visually pleasing. Fill a ziplock bag with the oil, water, paint, and glitter. Close it and seal it with packing tape.
- Because the components will remain separate from one another, this is both a multitextured experience and visually soothing. Before meals

and snacks, encourage children to trace lines, letters, and shapes or just mix the contents around for a fun, clean, visually pleasing sensory experience that supports the successful engagement in a textured activity.
- Another example is a sensory bag composed of hair gel and pompoms in varying sizes. This also provides a multitextured experience that is visually pleasing. As they manipulate the sensory bag, children can sort the pompoms by size or color. Or they can make patterns with the pompoms, pushing them with their fingers through the gel.

Messy Play with Sensory Trays

Alongside their peers, encourage children to engage in individual messy tactile play to decrease sensitivity to the look and feel of textures. This approach lets them interact with tactile input in a small, contained space that they have complete control over.

Intended outcomes:

- Learning to tolerate the look and feel of messy textures
- Learning how to stay calm and wipe their hands clean when they get messy
- Interacting with messy textures in a way that is not displeasing
- Learning that they are in control of their thoughts and feelings

Materials:

Paper plates or small baking sheets

Shaving cream or fingerpaint

Glitter, pompoms, and other add-ins (optional)

Non-latex gloves

Spoons

Paintbrushes

What to Do:

- Unlike a sensory bag, which is made ahead of time, a sensory tray is made in real time in front of the children. The base should be something messy but easy to put on the tray, such as shaving cream or fingerpaint. Add-ins are optional with sensory trays.
- Because this is an individual messy tactile activity, children who are sensitive to the feel of the base may use paintbrushes, gloves, or spoons to avoid getting their hands too messy.
- Before snack, during circle time, or seated at a table, make the sensory tray. Encourage children to interact with this tactile activity as they choose. Let them know that there is no right or wrong way to play, and help them to use their imaginations while they interact with the sensory tray.

Fingerpainting

Fingerpainting is an excellent messy tactile activity to help picky eaters stay calm and in control of themselves during snacks and meals.

Intended outcomes:

- Learning to tolerate the look and feel of messy textures
- Learning to stay calm and wipe their hands clean when they get messy
- Learning to interact with messy textures in a way that is not displeasing
- Learning that they are in control of their thoughts and feelings

Materials:

Fingerpaint

Small cups

Paper

Easel or table

Marbles, toy vehicles

Shaving cream, glitter, or sand

Non-latex gloves

Spoons

Paintbrushes

What to Do:

- Fill small cups with fingerpaint in a variety of colors. Set out the paint and paper on easels or on a table. Children may fingerpaint seated at the table as a small group activity or work on an easel as a center choice before snack or mealtime.
- Encourage them to explore by using as many colors and patterns as they want while feeling the cool, squishy texture of the paint. If needed, they might wear gloves or use a spoon or paintbrush to engage with the materials
- To encourage them to play longer, give them marbles that they can roll through the paint. Or give them toy cars and trucks and encourage them to make roads.
- Vary the texture by adding shaving cream, glitter, or sand to the paint. The longer children can engage in fingerpainting, the more accustomed they will become to the tactile experience and the more regulated they will be when they face similar textures during mealtimes.

Movement Strategies to Support Seated Attention and Focus during Mealtimes

To support sustained attention during mealtime, implement the following strategies before, during, and after meals and snacks. Children who struggle to pay attention during mealtimes may demonstrate out-of-control behaviors, including impulsivity, decreased concentration, the inability to stay on task, and the inability to follow directions. Instead of sitting quietly at the table, engaging with their peers, and focusing on their meal, these children get out of their seats frequently, disrupting the whole class. To help children sustain their attention for the duration of the meal, employ movement and proprioception activities throughout the school day.

Freeze Dance

Three- to five-minutes before snack time, during circle time, and before lunchtime, engage the children in this fun musical activity.

Intended outcomes:

- Engagement in movement input
- Improved attentional flexibility and working memory
- Improved inhibitory control

Materials:

Recorded music

What to Do:

- Ask the children to stand up and spread out a little so they do not run into each other.
- Tell them you will play music and they can dance any way they want to.
- When you stop the music, they have to freeze in place.
- When you restart the music, they can unfreeze and dance again.

Yoga Poses

Children who lack core strength may have difficulties with balance. These children may fall out of their chairs, fidget, or slump over the table because they need to move their bodies to engage the core muscles required to sit upright for a sustained period. Yoga poses help children develop concentration, balance, core strength, and stability. Poses such as the tree pose, downward dog, and table pose require focus and concentration as children pay attention to how to position their bodies correctly to assume the pose and then maintain the position for a certain amount of time.

Intended outcomes:

- Maintaining balance positions to improve their core strength and stability
- Improved inhibitory control

Materials:

No materials are required for yoga poses.

Optional materials include:

- Carpet squares or yoga mats
- YouTube videos such as Kids Yoga or Music and Mindfulness with Yo Re Mi
- Yoga cards, such as Yoga Pretzels Cards or Yoga for Littles

What to Do:

- During circle time or before snack, encourage the class to engage in a few minutes of yoga poses.
- Encourage them to follow along with a video or copy your poses.

Engaging in a few minutes of a movement activity that is focused and intentional before a sedentary activity such as snack or center time will not only improve student's core strength, it will also help them sustain their attention and focus better while seated.

Masking-Tape Tightrope Walk

This balance activity will help children strengthen their core muscles so they can participate in seated activities with less fidgeting and slumping.

Intended outcomes:

- Improved core strength and stability through maintaining balance positions
- Decreased fidgeting and slumping during seated activities
- Improved focus and balance

Materials:

Masking tape or painter's tape

What to Do:

- Place strips of masking or painter's tape in a variety of lengths on the floor.
- Before meals as a free-choice activity and during circle time, invite the children to walk on the tape lines without stepping off.

Sensory Activities to Support Emotional Regulation when Motor Skills Are Challenging

Children need well-developed fine-motor skills to be successful at serving themselves food, feeding themselves with a fork and spoon, and opening their food containers. Some children struggle to regulate their emotions when they spill or cannot open something on their own. When children practice scooping, pouring, dumping, and manipulating small objects during open-ended sensory play, they not only get practice with fine-motor skills but also learn important self-regulation skills for times when they spill, drop things, or make mistakes at mealtimes.

Caregivers can help children develop a toolbox of strategies to support self-regulation. For example, encourage and model positive self-talk such as, "It's okay. I'm still learning." Demonstrate a response after a spill: "Accidents happen. I'll just clean it up." Remind the children that it is okay to ask for help, make mistakes, and spill things.

> Alexa is one of the youngest in her prekindergarten class. She is friendly and loves imaginative play and storytelling. In general, she gets along well with her peers. At snack and mealtime, she often sits at the table with her lunch box unopened, waiting for a teacher to open it and set up her lunch. She watches the other children as they pour water from the community pitcher, still waiting for an adult to help her. Alexa does not regulate her emotions well during snack and mealtime. When she tries to pour

> water for herself from the pitcher, she often misses her cup and the water spills all over the table. This tends to make her cry or lash out at the classmates sitting next to her.
>
> Ms. Cindy, the teacher's aide, places spare bowls, spoons, measuring cups, and plastic food in the classroom's sensory table. She makes a colorful sign that says "Pre-K Kitchen Open for Business." During circle time, Ms. Cindy introduces the class to the new center activity and describes how children might play in this area. She reminds them that it is okay to spill and make mistakes there, and she shows them where paper towels and other cleaning items are if they do happen to spill.

In this example, Ms. Cindy has developed an open-ended sensory experience designed to help Alexa and the other children improve their fine-motor skills. She has provided the class with self-regulation strategies to use if things go wrong. Although she created this sensory activity with Alexa in mind, all children in the classroom will benefit from the pre-K kitchen.

Sand and Water Play

Sand and water play stations provide a great opportunity to practice fine-motor skills, such as passing, pouring, and scooping. With support from a caregiver, children can learn positive self-talk and other self-regulation strategies when they spill.

Intended outcomes:

- Developing self-regulation strategies
- Improved fine-motor skills

Materials:

Plastic bins or sand-and-water tables

Play sand

Water

Scoops, pitchers, pails, measuring cups, ladles

Paper towels

What to Do:

- Set up the sand-and-water table or bins, and add the tools and accessories.
- Encourage the children to explore the center.
- When they spill or become frustrated, give them the positive language to respond such as, "That's okay. Let's get a paper towel and wipe that up," or "I can see you're frustrated. Could you try passing the pitcher to her again?"

Cooking-Themed Sensory Bin

Transform sensory bins into an opportunity to develop fine-motor skills.

Intended outcomes:

- Developing self-regulation strategies to cope with spills or mistakes
- Improved fine-motor skills specific to scooping, pouring, and dumping
- Becoming comfortable interacting with eating utensils

Materials:

Plastic bins

Sand

Spoons, colanders, funnels, cups, plastic bottles, and bowls

What to Do:

- Start with a dry base such as sand. Add funnels, spoons, small colanders, measuring cups, and bowls.
- During free play or center time, encourage the children to become chefs and "cook" something with the materials in the bin. They can interact with just the base by scooping and pouring it while pretending they are baking or cooking a meal.

Food-Themed Treasure Hunt

Provide opportunities for children to improve their hand strength and fine-motor skills.

Intended outcomes:

- Developing self-regulation strategies to cope when they spill or make mistakes
- Improved fine-motor skills required to be independent and successful during mealtime
- Developing hand and finger strength
- Becoming comfortable interacting with eating utensils

Materials:

Plastic bin

Sand

Pompoms

Tongs

Small plastic food items

Tweezers

Spoons

Bowls

What to Do:

- Pour play sand into the bin. Add in small items such as pompoms and plastic food. Provide tweezers, tongs, and spoons.
- During free play or center time, encourage the children to pick up the items in the sand with spoons, tweezers, or tongs and place them into a bowl.
- Once all the items have been removed, the children may dump everything back into the bin and do another treasure hunt.

Co-Regulation during Snacks and Meals

The caregiver has an important role in helping children develop strong self-regulation skills during mealtimes. Creating a classroom environment that is calm and free of distractions will promote an atmosphere in which children can practice their self-help skills, social interactions, and communication.

Young children may need continual reminders to draw from prior experiences and support self-regulation during meals. Make connections between what they are eating and a sensory activity they participated in earlier in the day. For example, remind children who played in a sensory bin about the different textures they interacted with, and encourage them to identify foods with similar textures. Remind children how they regulated their emotions and shared limited resources as they engaged in messy sensory play, and suggest that they employ those same strategies during snacks and mealtime. Model the ways children can use the skills they demonstrated in sensory play earlier in the day to stay calm and in control and enjoy the experience of sharing a meal with their classmates.

Chapter 7:

In Control during Circle Time

Circle time is an important part of the school day when children and teachers gather to learn and share as a whole class, participating in the same activities at the same time. Children must be well regulated to pay attention to the person speaking, wait their turn, and feel comfortable sharing and engaging in a large group. Some teachers use circle time to begin and end each day, while others use it as a time to read stories, manage the classroom, communicate rules and routines, and work on social skills.

During circle time, children need strong self-regulation skills to:

- Inhibit their desire to talk out of turn
- Keep their hands to themselves
- Wait patiently to be called on
- Stay attentive while others are talking
- Tune out distractions
- Listen to and follow instructions
- Manage their emotions

As long as activities last for an age-appropriate amount of time, young children should be able to sit and attend for the duration of circle time. Often, it is the length of the individual activities, not the total length of circle time, that causes them to lose attention. For example, it is unrealistic to expect a group of four- and five-year-olds to sit and listen quietly to a twenty-minute lesson. But if circle time consists of a combination of movement breaks and engaging learning content, most young children can attend for the entire time.

> Kindergarten teacher Ms. Gigi has called the children to circle time. Each one transitions to the space and sits on an individual carpet square. Ms. Gigi welcomes them to class and asks how they are feeling. She allows a few children to share. Next, she taps the small gong that sits on her desk and asks the children to see how long they can hear the sound. She pulls out a book about feelings that shows characters feeling happy, shy, frustrated, scared, silly, and angry. She encourages the children to describe times they've experienced those emotions. Next, Ms. Gigi presents the group with a large feather and explains that she found it while on a hike over the weekend. She passes it to the student next to her and instructs him to pass it to the person next to him. While the children interact with the feather, Ms. Gigi introduces the learning topic for the week, animals and nature. She taps the gong again, encouraging the children to close their eyes to see how long they can hear the sound. Before transitioning away from circle time, Ms. Gigi gives instructions for the seated activity the children will work on next.

In this example, Ms. Gigi uses the gong to encourage seated attention. She encourages active listening while she reads the story. She uses the feather to help children stay engaged while she introduces the new learning module. Passing the feather encourages some movement. Ms. Gigi has used auditory input, visual input, and movement to help the children actively participate for the duration of circle time.

Auditory cues are excellent strategies for helping children transition to circle time. Common auditory cues include songs or chants such as, "Now it's time to listen. Listen . . . listen . . . listen"; a chime or drumbeat;

or a clapping pattern that children respond to with the same or a complementary clap. Using a well-established auditory cue for transitions helps children with attentional flexibility. They regulate their emotions to stop the activity they are engaged in and remember what the auditory signal means and where they are transitioning to next. Then, they independently transition to circle time with their peers.

Maintain a consistent circle-time routine. Be predictable. Plan circle time so it always follows the same order. When children know what to expect, they tend to be better at regulating their emotions. However, adding a new challenge to a well-known circle-time activity will keep children engaged. When they lose interest in an activity, impulsive behaviors will increase.

Structure circle time in this sequence each day:

- Opening listening activity (1 to 3 minutes) such as:
    - A chime or sound children listen to until they can no longer hear it
    - A good-morning song
    - A rhythmic drumbeat children copy with their hands or feet
- Learning activity (3 to 5 minutes) to introduce a learning module or talk about the weather
    - Make it interactive with manipulatives
    - Provide passive movement input
- Movement break (1 to 3 minutes) to improve inhibitory control and provide movement input to promote seated attention for the rest of circle time
    - Freeze dance
    - Yoga poses
- Learning activity or story time (5 to 10 minutes)
- Closing song and transition information (3 to 5 minutes) to help the children transition to the next part of the school day

The total length of circle time is between thirteen and twenty-six minutes, with lots of movement mixed in. Creating this kind of circle-time routine, with built-in flexibility, allows for more time spent in a movement activity when it's needed, or less time spent reading a book. There will be days when it feels impossible to hold the class's attention during circle time for just thirteen minutes, and days when twenty-plus minutes fly by. This routine encourages active listening and participation and supports a calm and in-control arousal level for all children for the duration of circle time.

Supports to Help Children Self-Regulate during Circle Time

Visual Supports

Visual supports help kindergartners with communicating, remembering class rules and routines, recognizing and respecting personal space, and transitioning. They help children gain control of their school day, decreasing frustration. Visual supports during circle time can define a space for each child. Use carpet pieces, tape, or other ways to mark the place where children belong while sitting together as a group. These visual reminders will help them control their desire to move around and distract others. And they allow those who crave personal space to gain control over their physical environment.

Post visual supports to help children remember the classroom rules and routine, referring to them often during circle time and encouraging the class to do the same. This encourages time management and helps children understand what comes next.

Movement Supports and Activities

It is hard for children to pay attention when they are seeking movement input by fidgeting, rolling around on the floor, or getting up from their place. Such movement is distracting to other children, diminishes the benefits of circle time, and makes it hard for children to regulate their emotions. Incorporating movement input into circle time will help the children pay attention to what they are learning and improve their self-regulation skills.

During circle time, children usually sit unsupported on the floor. For some, this is a difficult position to maintain because it requires more core strength and balance than sitting in a chair, where they have back and foot support to help keep them upright. Balance and proprioception activities throughout the school day will improve children's core strength and stability so that they are better able to sit unsupported during circle time.

Rather than attending to the circle-time activities, children who need core support to help them sit upright at circle time may fidget, roll around on the floor, lean on others, or lie on the floor.

Consider passive movement input for such children. Alternative seating options, such as a cushion, an inflatable wedge, a camp chair or stadium seat, or a beanbag chair, support both the children who have weak core muscles and those who crave movement during circle time. They also define the space they should occupy in the circle and help with focus and regulation. Offering cushions or inflatable wedges to children who seek movement allows them to move their bodies while seated so they can get the movement input they need while also participating in the circle-time activities.

To support attention and focus for the duration of circle time, incorporate songs, breaks, and learning activities. Movement at the start of circle time, partway through, and at the end will keep them focused on what they are learning. Freeze Dance is a great way to provide structured movement during whole-class activities. Children will improve their attentional flexibility, working memory, and inhibitory control by freezing their movements when the music stops and dancing while it plays. They will also improve their core strength and balance as they hold a specific position when they hear the music stop. Other activities to try include yoga poses and playing Simon Says.

Yoga Poses

Maintaining a yoga pose requires focus and balance. Participating will support children in developing their ability to pay attention and will develop their core strength.

Intended outcomes:

- Improved attention and focus during circle time
- Improved core strength and balance

Materials:

Carpet squares or yoga mats (optional)

Yoga cards

What to Do:

- During circle time, engage the children in a few minutes of yoga poses that encourage balance and stability. Children will need a visual model to properly execute each pose. They can copy you as you demonstrate each pose, or they can use yoga cards that show different poses.
- Popular yoga poses for children that they can do in a large group include tree pose, chair pose, mountain pose, downward dog, and table pose.

Simon Says

This classic game will provide structured movement and enhance children's listening skills.

Intended outcomes:

- Improved attentional flexibility, working memory, and inhibitory control
- Improved attention and focus
- Developing listening skills

What to Do:

- Ask the children to stand and to spread out in the circle-time space, so they do not bang into anyone.
- Explain that you will tell them to do a series of movements. They are to listen carefully and only do the movements that you say after saying "Simon says" (or use your name in place of *Simon*).
  For example, "Simon says take one step forward." "Simon says hop on one foot." "Touch the top of your head." The children would take one step forward, then hop on one foot. They would not touch the top of their heads.
- To play this in a noncompetitive way, and keep children from being "out," divide the children into two groups. When a child does something Simon didn't say, they simply switch over to the other group. Alternatively, you can have that child join you for one turn, then go back to the group.

Tactile Input

Tactile input enhances learning and interaction. Adding a tactile component to circle-time lessons and activities can help children remain well regulated and attentive to what they are learning. It also helps them keep their hands to themselves. For example, if the lesson is about transportation, pass around a special car, train, or airplane. If children are learning about animals, pass around an animal pelt, antler, or stuffed animal for everyone to interact with.

Teaching about Feelings in Circle Time

Meeting as a group encourages children to share their thoughts, feelings, and beliefs with their classmates. At the same time, they learn to respect others' opinions, listen, and wait their turn to share, developing strong self-regulation skills. Try activities such as role-play with puppets or stuffed animals, playing games such as "Guess what I'm feeling," and reading books that focus on feelings.

Role-Play to Support Dealing with Strong Emotions

Role-play with puppets or stuffed animals helps children work through big emotions. By exploring how a stuffed animal might feel in a stressful situation, children learn new ways to remain calm and in control of their feelings and behaviors the next time a situation arises. Common themes to role-play during circle time might include the following:

- When your paper rips while you're working on it
- When you don't get called on first
- When a pencil breaks
- When you really want to share but the teacher is occupied

To role-play with children during circle time, gather a variety of puppets or stuffed animals children can work with. Model how to role-play by pretending to be one of the puppets or stuffed animals with a big problem. Choose a student to be the teacher to help the puppet resolve the issue. Talk with the class about how the puppet feels and solutions it could use the next time it encounters the situation. Then, play the game again with a new issue.

Games to Support Understanding Feelings

Another circle-time idea to support strong self-regulation skills is to play games that teach feelings and emotions.

Guess What I'm Feeling

In this activity, either the teacher or a student will say an agreed-upon sentence with different emotions. The other children then guess what emotion the speaker is feeling. For example, start with a sentence such as, "I think it is raining outside." Model saying the sentence for the children in a neutral voice. Then say it in a way that expresses an emotion, such as angry, sad, inquisitive, happy, and so on. Encourage the children to guess the emotion, either by calling on them one by one or allowing them to raise their hands as a group to vote on what the emotion is.

Choose a volunteer in the circle to restate the sentence using a different emotion. Continue with the guessing game until all children have had a chance to lead the group.

Charades

Charades is a great game for teaching children about feelings and emotions.

Intended outcomes:

- Developing ability to recognize different emotions
- Improved ability to name emotions

Materials:

Hat or basket

Emotion faces

What to Do:

- Print out or draw faces showing different emotions: happy, mad, sad, curious, shy, sick, worried, afraid, tired, jealous, and so on. Place the emotion faces in a hat or basket.
- At circle time, pass the basket to a child seated in the circle. Encourage that student to remove a face and act out the feeling for the rest of the class to guess. Whisper what the emotion is if the student isn't sure.
- The student who guesses the correct emotion first goes next. Continue until every student who wants to has had a chance to act out an emotion.

Read Books about Emotions

Read books that focus on feelings, such as the following:

The Rabbit Listened by Cori Doerrfeld
Daniel's Good Day by Micha Archer

Evelyn Del Rey Is Moving Away by Meg Medina
Otto Goes to School by Todd Parr
A Little Spot of Feelings by Diane Alber
Positive Ninja by Mary Nhin
Owl Babies by Martin Waddell

Big Al by Andrew Clements
Hippos Go Berserk! by Sandra Boynton
Rex Wrecks It! by Ben Clanton
Can I Play Too? by Mo Willems
In My Heart by Jo Witek

Pause while reading and ask the children to reflect on how a character feels. If there is time, ask them to talk about times when they've felt this way. Discuss what they felt and why they felt it.

When you choose books with characters who break the classroom rules, such as *Rex Wrecks It!*, encourage a discussion about what the main character does, whether it is an appropriate reaction, and what the children would do in a similar situation. This helps the children think about strong reactions. They can learn that people feel big emotions sometimes and that there are right ways and wrong ways to react to them. Children learn self-regulation strategies by thinking of how the characters in the book react as opposed to how they should react.

Supporting Self-Regulation through Reflection

Circle time is an excellent opportunity to reflect as a group on the self-regulation skills children use throughout the school day. The classroom teacher can spend a few moments of circle time discussing the feelings, actions, and positive interactions she observed during the day. Children can also choose to talk about the positive things they noticed through the day in themselves or others.

> At the end of the school day, Ms. Patel calls the children to the carpet for their afternoon circle time, which she calls "Together Time." Once the children have finished their active-listening activity, Ms. Patel models language to describe what she heard

and observed in class that day. She says, "Today, I saw many children remembering and following our class rules. I saw a lot of sharing, heard a lot of kind words, and observed many children playing nicely with their friends." She looks around the circle, recognizing the whole class as active members who have contributed to the success of the school day. She continues with a specific example: "I want to give a special shout out to Emmet." She pauses for a moment, allowing the class to clap or snap for Emmet. "This morning, I saw Emmet use patience and kindness. I watched him share his favorite car with Eli while they were playing at the building and construction center. After Eli played with the car for a while, I listened to Emmet use his words to ask if he could have a turn with the car. Great job, Emmet!" Ms. Patel encourages the children to acknowledge Emmet by clapping or snapping their fingers. Then, she asks them if they observed a positive action during the day that they'd like to share.

This activity not only supports self-regulation and executive function skills, it also shows the class that these are important skills and are valued in the classroom.

Circle time is a beloved and important part of many school days. It allows children and teachers to gather as a class to learn and share. It is a time during which children must be well regulated to pay attention to the person speaking, wait their turn, and feel comfortable sharing and engaging in a large group. For some children, to remain calm and in control of their bodies and emotions during circle time is a challenge. Good classroom management and sensory strategies are important tools to implement to ensure a successful circle-time experience. Furthermore, circle time is an excellent opportunity to practice and reflect as a group on the self-regulation skills children use throughout the school day. By supporting and discussing self-regulation as a class, children can learn to recognize and value self-regulation in themselves and in others.

Chapter 8:

Calm and in Control While Learning

Whether children are learning as a whole group, in small-group teacher-directed instruction, through open-ended play during centers, or while playing outside, they need strong self-regulation skills to:

- Share limited resources
- Remain patient while waiting their turn
- Problem solve
- Play cooperatively
- Play by the rules
- Respect themselves and others
- Resolve conflicts
- Take turns on playground equipment
- Manage their time

Practicing these skills can cause big emotions, and children need to be well regulated to prevent meltdowns, tantrums, or aggressive behavior. Because they have more independence during center time, children must rely more on their executive function and self-regulation skills to remain calm and in control while they explore, learn, and interact with their classmates. Embedding sensory inputs throughout learning blocks will help all children achieve this goal.

Calm during Centers

Center time is a common part of the school day in preschool, prekindergarten, and kindergarten. During center time, children engage in activities in small groups located around the classroom. In addition to increasing their knowledge base, center time helps them learn problem-solving skills, social skills, attentional flexibility, inhibitory control, and working-memory skills as they engage in activities and remember classroom rules and routines.

Typically, center activities are led by the children. Rather than engaging in a teacher-driven activity in which they must follow explicit directions, children can seek what they want to interact with and explore the activity the way they want. Child-led centers are also naturally rich with sensory input. Children are learning by doing, and they are on the move while they actively explore and socialize. They learn in parallel with their peers or develop problem-solving and social skills when they work cooperatively to bring an idea to life. Child-led centers foster independence, allow children to express themselves, teach problem-solving skills, and develop self-regulation skills.

Centers are a great place for children to make mistakes and practice skills. Offering open-ended explorations shifts the focus of the activity from product oriented to process oriented. When there is no end point or right or wrong way to engage in center activities, children can try new things without the threat of failure. When the explorations are child led, children's prolonged engagement enhances focus, curiosity, and problem-solving skills, and children are better able to maintain control over their emotions when they do make a mistake.

Just because centers are open-ended does not mean there are no rules. Children must still follow the classroom rules and any others specific to the center they are working in. Visual and verbal reminders of these rules should be prominent throughout center time.

Open-ended centers may be especially challenging for children who struggle with attentional flexibility. These children may become upset if they don't know how to engage with center activities without specific steps or rules. They will benefit from prompts or suggestions to help them get started with an open-ended center activity. They may also need reminders that, as long as no classroom rules are broken, there is no right or wrong way to use center materials.

Children who are inflexible thinkers may have difficulty with open-ended centers because they believe there is a right and wrong way to engage with materials. These children may cry, tell on friends, and argue during activities when they perceive that another student "isn't doing it the right way." As they learn strategies to expand their point of view and become more flexible, they may need sensory supports to help them regain control of their emotions when they become upset. Encouraging them to visit the serene sensory space is one way to help them calm down and get control of their emotions.

Enhancing Centers with Sensory Inputs

Enhancing center activities with sensory inputs ensures that every child gets the most out of this part of the school day. Some may learn best with a hands-on approach, others may be visual learners, and others may need to have their bodies in motion. Multisensory activities—those that involve more than one sense—not only pique children's curiosity but also enhance learning and skill acquisition. When center activities are multisensory, children have multiple ways to connect with materials and topics. The more engaged children are, the less likely they will become bored or frustrated when they make a mistake. This allows them to remain well regulated throughout center time.

> Ms. Hoffman has noticed that many of her kindergartners avoid the writing center. Typically, children sit there and practice writing sight words. One morning, Ms. Hoffman decides to enhance the writing center with tactile materials to entice the children to go there and complete the sight-word activity. Along with paper and pencils, she adds a sensory bag filled with blue hair gel so children can trace their sight words. She

adds a baking tray filled with colored sand where children can write words with their fingers. And she adds playdough so children can form sight words from the clay. With these options, Ms. Hoffman has turned the writing center into a multisensory experience.

Before center time begins, Ms. Hoffman shows the class what's new in the writing center. She reminds them that the purpose of the writing center is to practice their sight words. Then, she shows them how they can use the new materials to trace, draw, and mold their sight words rather than just writing them out on the paper. By the end of the week, the writing center has become one of the children's favorites.

In Mr. Williams's preschool class, only a few children use the building center, which has a set of wooden blocks, some cars and trucks, and a bridge. Mr. Williams knows that building with blocks helps children develop math skills, problem-solving, creativity, and social skills, and he wants more of the children to enjoy going to this center. He decides to add colorful blocks, textured blocks, and plastic blocks that rattle when shaken. Before center time begins, Mr. Williams shows the class what's new in the building center and demonstrates how they can build castles, cities, and towers. He passes around some of the new blocks and challenges the children to create something from their imaginations. When center time begins, many children rush to the building center, which has been transformed into a multisensory experience.

Sensory Center Choices

Tactile sensory centers, such as art centers, sensory tables, and sensory bins, help children learn important self-regulation skills that they will rely on throughout the school day. For example, picky eaters learn coping strategies they can use during mealtimes. All children improve their fine-motor skills, which reduces frustration with learning to hold and manipulate writing utensils and other tools. The materials support and encourage children's self-expression and provide opportunities for problem solving as they bring their ideas to life. Teachers will need to be on hand while children engage in tactile sensory centers to offer advice, compliment good self-regulation skills, and remind children to use their skills to remain calm and in control of their emotions.

Some children will benefit from visiting the serene sensory space during center time so they can calm down and work on self-regulation when their emotions get the better of them. This space should be considered a center choice that children can visit whenever they need to.

Using Sensory Inputs to Support Time Management and Transitions

Children may struggle with time management and transitions during center time, causing them to become defiant and upset. These behaviors are disruptive to the whole class and take time away from this important part of the day. Time management is hard for young children because their sense of time has not fully developed. Visual and auditory supports designed to help them understand the passage of time will support them in remaining calm and in control when one center ends and they transition to the next one.

Visual Supports

Visual supports are excellent tools to help children independently transition from one center to the next and manage their time during center activities. When children understand how much time they have to complete an activity or know how long they have to wait before the next center begins, they are better able to remain calm during the activity, clean up when it is time to finish, and smoothly transition to the next activity.

> Ms. Nicole knows that center time is one of the most beloved parts of the day for her preschoolers. She also knows that this is a time when many self-regulation difficulties arise as the children share toys; transition from one center to the next; and manage their time to play, socialize, and learn. Ms. Nicole uses multiple visual aids to help the children remain calm and in control of their emotions. She labels each center area with the name of the center and a

sign-up sheet. This lets children know what the center is, helps them understand what they might do there, and limits the number of children in one area. Children sign in by velcroing a laminated picture of themselves to the sign-in sheet. Ms. Nicole sets an auditory time for ten minutes so the whole class is aware of when they will switch center activities. Within each center, she has visual timers available to help manage conflict between children or to help individual children know when it is time to clean up and transition to the next activity. Once children have transitioned to the next center, the visual timer can start again. Ms. Nicole uses these visual timers throughout center time to help children share toys, wait their turn, and transition when it is time to. In this way, the children have a sense of control over their surroundings, learn to manage their time, and understand that they need to wait their turn patiently.

Auditory Supports

Auditory cues, such as songs, chimes, and chants, are useful sensory tools to help children manage their time and transition between activities. To be effective, teachers will need to teach and use these tools consistently. Once the children understand what the cue means, they will be better able to control their emotions during transitions.

Ms. Watson has thirty children in her pre-K class. Center time is an enjoyable part of the school day, but it is loud and tends to be chaotic when children transition from one center to the next. Kyra regularly lags behind and often becomes upset because she hasn't finished what she is working on. At times, she refuses to clean up and transition to the next center, causing a disruption to the whole class.

Each day, Ms. Watson uses a small metal gong to call the children to morning meeting, and she decides to use the gong to help Kyra and her classmates manage their time during centers. Before center time begins, she calls the children to the carpet to explain her idea. First, she tells them that when they hear the gong chime during centers, it means that it is time to clean up. She reminds them of the importance of cleaning up for the next group of children. Then, she lets a few children try the gong and announce in a loud voice, 'Cleanup time." Next, she chooses Kyra to oversee the announcement of cleanup time during centers. Finally, she dismisses the class from the carpet to start their first center activity.

Ms. Watson tells the class that it will be time to clean up in five minutes, making sure Kyra has heard. Quietly, she reminds Kyra of her job. Ms. Watson gives a one-minute reminder to the class and motions for Kyra to meet her at the gong. Kyra waits for the final minute to pass, bangs the gong, and announces, "Cleanup time." Before she returns to her group, Ms. Watson praises Kyra for helping and reminds her how important it is for everyone to start a center together, clean up the area, and then transition to the next center together.

Teacher-Directed Learning Blocks

Some blocks of learning time in the prekindergarten and kindergarten classrooms will be teacher directed rather than child led. These learning blocks are often product driven, with the teacher in charge of teaching specific course material to a small group of children.

When executed for short periods of time, teacher-directed learning is an effective method to teach important literacy, science, and math content and to ensure that all children are learning key material. The teacher guides children's problem solving and task completion, allowing children to practice recently learned skills and receive feedback and guidance in the moment. In this learning style, children can work on self-regulation and executive function to problem solve, plan, and complete a task.

Self-regulation difficulties rarely occur during small-group learning blocks. These learning opportunities tend to be highly structured, with a low student-to-teacher ratio, and as long as they are not too long, children should be able to remain calm and in control for the full time. If they do struggle to remain well regulated during teacher-directed learning, children are usually seeking movement input, are bored with the activity, or are upset that someone else is being called on. This is when sensory supports come in handy.

It may be hard for some children to pay attention during teacher-directed learning if they seek movement input. They may fall out of their chairs, fidget in their seats, or get up and move around the classroom. This is distracting to other children and may make it hard for the others in the group to regulate their emotions. Alternative seating options that provide movement input will allow these children to pay attention to what they are learning. Common alternative seating options include:

- Sitting on an exercise ball instead of a regular chair
- Sitting on an inflatable cushion on a school chair
- Sitting on T-stools

Children who struggle to sit still and focus during teacher-directed learning activities may benefit from tactile sensory inputs, as some children learn best with a hands-on approach. Adding a tactile component to learning activities will help children pay attention. For example, encourage children to learn math skills with a hands-on approach, such as adding and subtracting Legos, blocks, chenille stems, or wood sticks. Let them string beads to work on patterning and counting. Let them write letters and numbers in shaving cream or sand. Hide learning materials in sensory bins for children to find before they can use them. Form words, shapes, and patterns with modeling clay or playdough.

Embedding sensory inputs throughout teacher-directed learning blocks will help children with different types of learning styles remain calm and in control of their emotions so they can focus on the day's lessons.

References and Recommended Reading

American Academy of Pediatrics, American Public Health Association, National Resource Center for Health and Safety in Child Care and Early Education. 2011. *Caring for Our Children: National Health and Safety Performance Standards; Guidelines for Early Care and Education Programs.* 3rd edition. Elk Grove Village, IL: American Academy of Pediatrics.

Anzman-Frasca, Stephanie, Lori A. Francis, and Leann L. Birch. 2015. "Inhibitory Control is Associated with Psychosocial, Cognitive, and Weight Outcomes in a Longitudinal Sample of Girls." *Translational Issues in Psychological Science* 1(3): 203–216.

Ayres, A. Jean. 1972. *Sensory Integration and Learning Disorders.* Los Angeles: Western Psychological Services.

Barkley, Russell A. 2010. "Differential Diagnosis of Adults with ADHD: The Role of Executive Function and Self-Regulation." *The Journal of Clinical Psychiatry* 71(7): e17.

Bestbier, Lana, and Timothy I. Williams. 2017. "The Immediate Effects of Deep Pressure on Young People with Autism and Severe Intellectual Difficulties: Demonstrating Individual Differences." *Occupational Therapy International.* DOI:10.1155/2017/7534972

Boyce, Peter, et al. 2006. "Lighting Quality and Office Work: Two Field Simulation Experiments." *Lighting Research and Technology* 38(3): 191–223.

Bundy, Anita C., Sue Shia, Long Qi, and Lucy Jane Miller. 2007. "How Does Sensory Processing Dysfunction Affect Play?" *The American Journal of Occupational Therapy* 61(2): 201–208.

Burdette, Hillary L., and Robert C. Whitaker. 2005. "Resurrecting Free Play in Young Children: Looking Beyond Fitness and Fatness to Attention, Affiliation, and Affect." *Archives of Pediatric and Adolescent Medicine* 159(1): 46–50.

Chen, Hsin-Yung, Hsiang Yang, H.-J. Chi, and H.M. Chen. 2013. "Physiological Effects of Deep Touch Pressure on Anxiety Alleviation: The Weighted Blanket Approach." *Journal of Medical and Biological Engineering* 33(5): 463–470.

Cowan, Nelson. 2014. "Working Memory Underpins Cognitive Development, Learning, and Education." *Educational Psychology Review* 26(2): 197–223.

Galyer, Karma T., and Ian M. Evans. 2001. "Pretend Play and the Development of Emotion Regulation in Preschool Children." *Early Child Development and Care* 166(1): 93–108.

Harms, Thelma, Richard M. Clifford, and Debby Cryer. 2014. *Early Childhood Environment Rating Scale.* 3rd edition. New York: Teachers College Press.

Hofmann Wilhelm, Brandon J. Schmeichel, and Alan D. Baddeley. 2012. "Executive Functions and Self-Regulation." *Trends in Cognitive Sciences* 16(3):174–80.

Howard-Jones, Paul, Jayne Taylor, and Lesley Sutton. 2002. "The Effect of Play on the Creativity of Young Children during Subsequent Activity." *Early Child Development and Care* 172(4): 323–328.

Howard, Steven J., and Elena Vasseleu. 2020. "Self-Regulation and Executive Function Longitudinally Predict Advanced Learning in Preschool." *Frontiers in Psychology* 11: 49. DOI:10.3389/fpsyg.2020.00049

Losinski, Mickey, Sara A. Sanders, and Nicole M. Wiseman. 2016. "Examining the Use of Deep Touch Pressure to Improve the Educational Performance of Children with Disabilities: A Meta-Analysis." *Research and Practice for Persons with Severe Disabilities* 41(1): 3–18.

McClelland, Megan, Sara Schmitt, and Shauna Tominey. May 28, 2013. "Improving Self-Regulation in Young Children through Circle Time Games." Paper presented at Society for Prevention Research 22nd Annual Meeting, San Francisco, CA.

McGinnis, Amy A., et al. 2013. "The Behavioral Effects of a Procedure Used by Pediatric Occupational Therapists." *Behavioral Interventions* 28(1): 48–57.

Montroy, Janelle J., et al. 2016. "The Development of Self-Regulation across Early Childhood." *Developmental Psychology* 52(11): 1744–1762.

Murray, Desiree W., Katie Rosanbalm, Christina Christopoulos, and Amar Hamoudi. 2015. *Self-Regulation and Toxic Stress: Foundations for Understanding Self-Regulation from an Applied Developmental Perspective.* OPRE Report #2015-21. Washington, DC: Office of Planning, Research and Evaluation, Administration for Children and Families, U.S. Department of Health and Human Services.

Pellegrini, Anthony D. 1980. "The Relationship between Kindergartners' Play and Achievement in Prereading, Language, and Writing." *Psychology in the Schools* 17(4): 530–535.

Pianta, Robert C., Karen M. La Paro, and Bridget K. Hamre. 2007. *Classroom Assessment Scoring System Manual: Pre–K.* Baltimore, MD: Paul H. Brookes.

Russ, Sandra W., and Claire E. Wallace. 2013. "Pretend Play and Creative Processes." *American Journal of Play* 6(1): 136–148.

Schmeichel, Brandon J., Rachael N. Volokhov, and Heath A. Demaree. 2008. "Working Memory Capacity and the Self-Regulation of Emotional Expression and Experience." *Journal of Personality and Social Psychology* 95(6): 1526–1540.

Smolders, Karin C. H. J., and Yvonne A. W. de Kort. 2013. "Bright Light and Mental Fatigue: Effects on Alertness, Vitality, Performance and Physiological Arousal." *Journal of Environmental Psychology* 39: 77–91.

Tarle, Stephanie J., R. Matt Alderson, Elaine F. Arrington, and Delanie K. Roberts. 2019. "Emotion Regulation and Children with Attention-Deficit/ Hyperactivity Disorder: The Effect of Varying Phonological Working Memory Demands." *Journal of Attention Disorders* 25(6): 851–864.

Watts, Tara, Karen Stagnitti, and Ted Brown. 2014. "Relationship between Play and Sensory Processing: A Systematic Review." *The American Journal of Occupational Therapy* 68(2): e37–e46.

Index

A

Active listening skills, 61–62, 85, 91

Addition and subtraction, 65, 104

Aggressive behavior, 12, 31, 97

Attention and focus, 2, 63–65, 76–79, 85, 89

Attentional flexibility, 21–25, 31, 53, 58, 61–64, 87, 89, 98–99

Attentional inhibition, 30, 59

Auditory inputs/supports, 49–50

and play, 39–41

circle time cues, 86–87

enhancing centers with, 102–103

exploring sound with sound tubes, 60–61

for classroom rules, 47

reducing distractions, 50

sound tubes, 40–41

to support self-regulation, 59–61

B

Balance, 43–44, 63–64, 77–79, 89–90

Blurting out answers, 3, 30–31

C

Calming children

during learning time, 97–104

during mealtimes, 69–83

serene sensory space, 64–65

tactile inputs, 64

Centers, 98–101

Challenging behaviors, 6, 8, 11–12

Cheating, 31

Children's books about emotions, 93–94

Big Al by Andrew Clements, 94

Can I Play Too? by Mo Willems, 94

Daniel's Good Day by Micha Archer, 93

Evelyn Del Rey Is Moving Away by Meg Medina, 94

Hippos Go Berserk! by Sandra Boynton, 94

In My Heart by Jo Witek, 94

A Little Spot of Feelings by Diane Alber, 94

Otto Goes to School by Todd Parr, 94

Owl Babies by Martin Waddell, 94

Positive Ninja by Mary Nhin, 94

The Rabbit Listened by Cori Doerrfeld, 93

Rex Wrecks It! by Ben Clanton, 94

Circle time, 10, 85–95

Clapping, 49–50, 54, 87

Class rules and routines
consistency, 8–10, 54
disregarding, 30
talking about, 54, 57–58
to support self-regulation, 5, 57–58
visual and auditory supports, 47–49, 88
Communication skills, 33
Conflict resolution, 97
Consistency, 8–10, 19, 54, 87
Cooperative play, 97
Core strength, 63–64, 78–79, 89–90
Co-regulation, 1, 6–7, 53–56, 82–83

D

Deep pressure activities, 44–45
Distractions, 50, 55
Dysregulated responses, 11–14

E

Eating utensils, 81–82
Empathy, 22
Environment, 8, 14–17, 19
auditory sensory inputs, 39–41
co-regulation with familiar adults, 53–56
fine- and gross-motor skills, 16–17
kindergarten classroom, 57–67
physical, 47–50
preschool/pre-K classroom, 47–56
rules to support self-regulation, 57–58
sensory inputs, 58–65
sensory rich, 66–67
sensory sensitivity, 14–16
sensory spaces, 51–53
Executive function, 21–22, 97
attentional flexibility, 21–25
impulse control, 21, 29–31
play and, 33
self-regulation and, 21–31
working memory, 21, 25–28

F

Feelings
books about, 93–94
games to support understanding, 92–93
identifying, 8, 10–11, 19, 34, 91–94
role-play, 92
teaching about in circle time, 91–94
validating, 10–11, 17–18
Fight-or-flight response, 11
Filtering information, 27
Fine-motor skills

center time, 100
cooking-themed sensory bin, 81
food-themed treasure hunt, 81–82
play and, 33
sand and water play, 80–81
sensory inputs, 58
sensory play, 16–17
sound tubes, 60–61
supporting emotional regulation, 79–82
tactile inputs, 64–65
tactile space, 53
Fingerpainting, 75–76
Flexible thinking, 23–25
Foods, 69–70
Food-themed treasure hunt, 81–82
Furniture arrangement, 47–48

G

Games
Charades, 93
Dance Along to Brain-Break Songs, 63–64
Duck, Duck, Goose, 42
Follow the Leader, 43, 67
Freeze Dance, 42, 63, 77, 87, 89
Freeze Tag, 45
Guess What I'm Feeling, 91–93
Hopscotch, 44
Hopscotch through the Hallway, 62
Literacy Scavenger Hunt, 43, 61–62
Red Light, Green Light, 42
scavenger hunts, 42–43
Simon Says, 89–91
that encourage attention and focus, 42
to support understanding feelings, 92–93
What Time Is It, Mr. Fox? 42
Gross-motor skills, 16–17, 33, 58

H

Hand and finger strength, 81–82
Heavy work activities, 44–45
Home life, 7

I

I Spy bags or bottles, 39
Identifying feelings, 8, 10–11, 19
books about, 93–94
games to support, 92–93
in circle time, 91–94
role-play, 92
through sensory play, 34
Impulse control, 2–3, 21, 29–31
attentional inhibition, 30

center time, 98
defined, 28
movement, 61, 63, 89
response inhibition, 30–31
role-play, 18–19
self-regulation and, 31
tactile space, 53
visual supports, 58
yoga poses, 77–78
Impulsivity, 12, 29
Independence, 5
center time, 98
Inflexible thinking, 23–25, 99
Inhibitory control. See Impulse control

K

Kids Yoga, 78
Koo Koo Kanga Roo, 42, 64

L

Language development, 58, 70
Learning time, 97–104
Lighting, 50
Lining up, 3
Literacy skills, 43, 61–62, 65

M

Making mistakes, 98
Masking-tape balance beams, 44
Memory. See Working memory
Messy play, 35–37
picky eaters, 70–71
sensory bags, 36–37
sensory bins, 35–36
sensory trays, 74–75
Modeling, 8, 17–19, 58–59
Movement
balance activities to support seated attention, 43–44
inputs, 61–64
obstacle courses, 42
seated attention and focus at mealtimes, 76–79
sensory play, 41–44
space for, 52–53
supports and activities at circle time, 88–91
tactile input, 91
Multisensory activities, 99
Music, 39–40, 50, 54, 60–61, 63–64, 66–67, 77

O

Organization skills, 2
Overly silly behaviors, 6

P

Passive movement, 67, 89

Patience, 12, 18–19, 30, 58–59, 85

Pattern recognition, 63–64

Persistence, 5

Personal space, 85, 88

Picky eaters, 70–80, 100

Playing by the rules, 97

Positive language, 57–58, 79–81, 94–95

Preschool/pre-K classroom, 47–56

Prior experiences, 7

Problem-solving skills, 5

- auditory supports, 59–60
- center time, 97–98
- executive function, 22
- scavenger hunts, 61–62
- sensory inputs, 58
- tactile inputs, 64
- tactile space, 53

Proprioception, 44–45, 89

R

Reducing distractions, 50

Reflection, 94–95

Regrouping, 3

Remembering multistep directions, 22

Respect, 97

Response inhibition, 30–31

Role-play, 18–19, 91

Ruminating, 24

Rushing schoolwork, 30

S

Sabotage, 31

Sand and water play, 80–81

Scavenger hunts, 42–43

Seated attention, 38–39, 43–44, 52, 76–79, 86

Self-monitoring, 22

Sensory bags/bins, 35–37, 71–74, 81

Sensory inputs, 58–65

- auditory, 59–61, 102–103
- enhancing centers with, 99–101
- movement, 61–64
- to support time management and transitions, 101–103
- visual, 58–59, 101–102

Sensory play, 8, 14–17, 19, 33–45, 79–82

- at mealtimes, 70–76
- auditory, 39–41
- benefits of, 34
- cooking-themed sensory bin, 81
- fine- and gross-motor skills, 16–17
- fingerpainting, 75–76
- food-themed treasure hunt, 81–82
- messy play with sensory trays, 74–75
- movement, 41–44

picky eaters, 70–71
proprioception, 44–45
sand and water play, 80–81
sensitivity, 14–16
sensory bags, 73–74
sensory bins, 61–73
tactile/messy, 35–37
visual, 37–39
Sensory spaces, 51–53, 64–65, 101
Sensory strategies to support self-regulation, 3
turn-taking, 3, 7, 22, 33, 70, 91, 97
sharing, 3, 33, 70, 97
lining up, 3
refraining from blurting out answers, 3
freedom from separation anxiety, 3
handling transitions, 3
regrouping, 3
impulse control, 3
socially appropriate behavior, 3
Sensory supports, 102–104
Sensory tables, 36
Sensory trays, 74–75
Sensory tubes, 38
Sensory-rich kindergarten classroom, 66–67
Serene sensory space, 51–52, 64–65, 101
Sharing, 3, 7, 33, 70, 97
Short-term memory. See Working memory
Social skills, 2, 5, 33, 53, 58, 61–62, 70, 98
Socially appropriate behavior, 3
Songs, 49, 64
Sound tubes, 40–41
Storytelling, 19
Stressors, 7
Student-to-teacher ratio, 103

T

Tactile inputs, 65, 91
Tactile play. See Messy play
Tactile space, 53
Taking turns. See Turn-taking
Talking, 7, 85
Tantrums, 6, 30, 97
Teacher-directed learning blocks, 103–104
Teaching self-regulation, 8–14
Temperament, 7
Tightrope walking, 78–79
Time management skills, 58–59, 97, 101–103
Timers, 48

Transitions, 3, 22, 58–59, 62, 66–67, 88, 99–100

Treasure hunts, 81–82

Turn-taking, 3, 7, 22, 33, 70, 91, 97

V

Validating feelings, 10–11, 17–18

Verbal reminders, 26

Visual distractions, 55

Visual sensory play, 37–39

Visual inputs/supports, 9, 26, 47–49, 57, 59, 88, 102–103

W

Withdrawal/hiding, 6, 12

Word and idea generation, 22

Working memory, 21, 25–28, 31, 59, 61, 63, 89, 98

Y

Yoga for Littles, 78

Yoga poses, 44–45, 77–78, 87, 89–90

Yoga Pretzels Cards, 78